PRIV

PRIVACY
AND HOW TO GET IT BACK

B.J. MENDELSON

For Wendy Morin
Mom, I love you, and I miss you every day.

CURIOUS READS

An imprint of URTEXT
Unit 6 53 Beacon Road
London SE13 6ED

ISBN 978-1-912475-01-8

CONTENTS

ACKNOWLEDGEMENTS

I want to thank the people who read early versions of this book and gave me feedback and suggestions. I wrote my first and second book (the ghostwritten one) mostly in a vacuum. So, I really enjoyed working collaboratively with people on this. My writing is much, much better for it. My head is a bad neighbourhood, as my friend Phil McCaleb describes it, and it's sometimes hard to continue writing because I just get into these moods where everything sucks and then nothing gets done for a month. Maybe longer. Having all of you around helped minimize that while I wrote and finished this book.

I want to thank my editor for first approaching me about writing this in the Fall of 2015, and then rescuing it from the black hole the manuscript vanished into to get it revised and released in 2017. I often told people that I wrote three books, but that they'll never get to read the third one. That's no longer the case.

I want to thank Mark Hopkins, Rebeca Easton, and the team at The Roger Wilco Agency (ro.gerwil.co) for giving this book the solid edits it needed, and Irina Gonzalez and Amanda King for doing the same. Finally, I want to thank Jackie Shantie, the love of my life in some other dimension, and the other Wonder Women in my life, past and present. They know who they are and what they mean to me. Especially Coco Steele, whom I met at the same time I started working on this book. A word of dating advice: any time you find someone willing to throw on a superheroine costume for you, and actually enjoys doing so, you should probably marry them.

B.J. Mendelson

CHAPTER ONE

YOUR WEBCAM TOLD YOU TO DO WHAT?!

What follows is a collection of essays about privacy written between the Fall of 2015 and the Fall of 2017. Everything was up to date as of October 2017, but stuff might have happened since. For example, I don't get too much into the Facebook/Russia brouhaha, because the Senate investigation was ongoing at the time that I handed this manuscript to the publisher, although in that specific case I think the Russian interference in the 2016 US presidential election through social media was completely overblown by traditional media organizations—all in the name of ratings, page views, and vapid justifications. It pains me to say that as a 'liberal communist pinko' (my Dad's definition of a Democrat) but it's the truth. If you're curious as to why, I encourage you to read my first book, *Social Media Is Bullshit*.

Although I could have written another 30,000 words

on just the advertising industry and its role in eroding your privacy while automating itself out of existence, most people don't care about that. (Also: Bob Hoffman beat me to it with his book *BadMen: How Advertising Went From a Minor Annoyance to a Major Menace*.) Well, most people don't care, beyond those who work in the industry. And they're not going to want to read this, or Bob's book either, because you can't go against the tide in that business. Even if you, working for an agency, know that putting money into Facebook advertisements can be like flushing money down the toilet, if your client walks in the room and pays you to use Facebook as an advertising platform because of all the data they have collected, you're going to smile and take the money.

On Facebook ads: Facebook's entire business proposition is that since they know so much about their users, it's more beneficial to advertise with them than with a high street broadcast network. The comedian Lewis Black has this great routine he does about how, when he goes to Vegas, he doesn't go onto the casino floor to gamble. Instead, he takes his quarters and flushes them down the toilet in his hotel room, since the odds are about the same of him winning on the casino floor as the toilet clogging up and giving him back all his money. That's Facebook advertising in a nutshell. Sure, sometimes Facebook ads work out great, but you probably could have spent the money on other, far less creepy and far more effective methods of advertising; advertising that your customers would like and, actually, remember. Which raises a lot of questions when you think about it. If Facebook is a (mostly) terrible advertising platform that utilizes reams of personal data, one might assume that someone would have caught on to this by now and said something… But few in the advertising and tech world listen to reason. Nor do they want to turn off the faucet of billions of dollars flowing their way, so your privacy continues to get wrecked at the expense of colossal greed and wilful ignorance.

But this isn't a book about social media and its lack of effectiveness, beyond pointing out that this flawed justification is often used to collect more and more of your data. This book is meant to inform you about what's being done with your data by billion-dollar tech companies like Facebook, and how those companies and others, like Equifax, are allowed to get away with creeping on you due to a lack of tools, processes, and legislation to protect you. If you're looking for an ethics debate about privacy, or want to discover why it's important to be concerned about all this because that's part of being a good citizen, this isn't the book. Like most Americans, I don't like the idea that companies are making billions off my personal data, but I also know that there's not much I can do to stop them, beyond what's discussed in this book. This is especially true if we want to maintain the convenience and ease of use that we enjoy with some of today's most popular apps and services. With the way 'big data' and most algorithms work, many of our favourite platforms and apps would not function well (if at all) if we dramatically curtailed the amount of information they could collect on us. Amazon, for example, can make great recommendations based on the things you've purchased and searched for, but you first have to actually go ahead and start your search with Amazon and purchase things through them to improve those recommendations. Likewise, just imagine how much fun Instagram would be if you didn't have any friends on there. There's a transaction that takes place between us and these platforms, but as I will show you, this transaction is comically lopsided—mostly for no other reason than because we allow it to be.

'Big data', by the way, rarely has a consistent definition that everyone agrees on. So I use 'data' and 'big data' interchangeably throughout this book. All 'big data' was meant to refer to, before it got co-opted by the marketing people, is the sheer amount of data being collected that far exceeds the amount of space available to put it. The most I can practically achieve is to educate you about what's going on. And if some of this sounds like common sense, that's great. Give this book to someone who needs to read it then.

As I've said in the past, common sense isn't actually that common. What may seem obvious to you and me, is rarely obvious to the person sitting next to you. And when it comes to privacy, there's real lack of education—especially so when it comes to data collection through Internet-enabled devices, which is what we'll focus on.

Privacy, as it relates to the Internet and data collection, is an ongoing discussion, and I want this book to be valuable for as long as that discussion needs to occur. That means that future editions of this book might be called for. If you want to help on that front, you can buy an extra copy of this book and share it with a friend or colleague who might be interested. You can also leave an honest review of this book on Amazon. I'm a believer in word-of-mouth marketing, and a big part of that is getting third-party testimonials. This way, if someone is browsing around for books on privacy, they'll stop and look at your reviews and consider ordering this book. Those reviews are also valuable to me because I plan to take all of your feedback from those reviews and address them in future editions. So, make sure to leave an honest review.

Before we get into things, I want to make a few points clear that I think will help you understand where I'm coming from:

1. What makes this book compelling, and unique among other books on privacy, is that it deals exclusively with something that's entirely within our power to fix. That is, dealing with the use and abuse of our data by companies like Alphabet, Amazon, Microsoft, Apple, and Facebook, in order to further their bottom line. If I'm successful, I'll have helped motivate you to contact your representatives to push for legislation and regulations that will hold these companies, and others, accountable for their use of your data. My hope is that the threat of regulation will force these companies to be more transparent and form an independent organization that holds them all to a high standard, and penalizes those companies that fail to meet it.

2. I wanted to write a book on privacy that was light on histrionics and morality and heavy on educating you about what's going on. I write in an intentionally exaggerated and aggressive way that doesn't come from spite, but from a desire to educate and entertain. So, if you notice me repeating a point or two, swearing, or saying something funny or ridiculous, this is intended as a way to get some

of the lessons found within this book ingrained deep inside your mind.

3. The 'why' of this book: your data is worth a fortune. Whether you actively use the Internet or not, the odds are that there's a data file on you out there, and companies and criminals will stop at nothing to get that data for a multitude of reasons we'll discuss. So, although I have no idea how it'll be implemented yet, I'm a big advocate of you getting paid an annual license fee, or a small daily payment, in exchange for your data by these and other companies. If you're really into cars, you should be able to sell your data to Tesla or the local dealership group, in exchange for seeing ads from them when you browse the Web. Or maybe you get compensated based on what you do. If you work in the online marketing business, and a company like Moz or Ahrefs wants your business, they could pay you in exchange for your time and attention. We don't need creepy companies collecting and selling our data without our consent and without compensating us. We just need the will to put this system in place.

Now, in a lot of books, readers don't make it beyond the first chapter. I hope that this won't be the case here, but I'd rather cover my ass just to be sure. For those of you who want to protect your data as you use Internet-enabled devices, the following are my suggestions on what free services and tools you can use.

None of these apps, websites, or programs are perfect. You need to understand that just by using the Internet, you've already surrendered your privacy in some form to your Internet Service Provider (ISP), to the company whose device you're using, and to the company who makes the browser you choose to use. What you can do is minimize the amount of data being collected, and at the time of this writing, the following tools are the best we've got for this.

(Also: always remember to update the software you're using (whether it's on your mobile device or on a desktop) and you should put some tape over your computer's camera, or any Internet-connected camera that you might have. That's the fastest, easiest thing you can do to protect your privacy, and it doesn't cost you much in terms of money and time. Do that right now, before moving on to the next chapter.)

WEB BROWSER: TOR
https://www.torproject.org/

Tor is not the most user-friendly Internet browser, but if you want the most security you can get for your web browsing, Tor is the one. Like everything else on this list, it's imperfect, but it's much better than all the alternatives. If I can't convince you to switch browsers, I can at the very least recommend you check out DuckDuckGo.com. It's a search engine that doesn't track you or store anything you've entered into it the way that Google does.

MESSAGING APP: SIGNAL
https://signal.org/

Do you remember when Snapchat first took off, and people were using it to send nude photos because they thought the photos were deleted for real after a certain period of time? Well, none of that was true, and these days we have plenty of messaging applications to trade naughty, and not-so-naughty, messages with each other securely, like Nude (nudeapp.co). But if you want to be able to send those (and other) messages securely, and use a service that actually does delete the data being sent from their servers, then Signal is the messaging app for you. Again, like Tor, Signal is not perfect, but given the choice between trusting Facebook's Messenger, WhatsApp, or any of the built-in operating system chat applications like Apple's iMessage, Signal is the best option at this time. (And don't forget to delete your nudes too. You don't want your favourite body parts to show up on an Apple TV screensaver when you have your parents over).

Adblocker: Privacy Badger
https://www.eff.org/privacybadger

Privacy Badger doesn't block all the ads. AdBlock Plus is a better choice on that front, but AdBlock used to be kind of skeezy in that they were, basically, blocking people's ads, and then extorting advertisers. They did this by saying that if you want your ads to get past their software, you have to pay them. They've since backed off from this and seem to be getting better, but that whole deal left a lot of people with a bad taste in their mouth. Privacy Badger, on the other hand, comes from the not-for-profit Electronic Frontier Foundation (EFF), which is by far the best privacy organization that's been around since the days of *Please Hammer, Don't Hurt 'Em*. So, they have the cred and, also, lack the profit incentive that others in the field currently suffer under. Privacy Badger also does curtail most of the annoying ads out there and even alerts you to the number of trackers and advertisements it's flagged.

One more thing on the advertising front: you can go to http://optout.aboutads.info/ and opt out of a lot of the online advertising networks that track you through your web browsing. It won't get you off all the data-sharing lists, but it's a good place to start. In addition, the Center for Internet and Society at Stanford University set up DoNotTrack.us, which can also provide you with information on how to limit the amount of tracking and data-gathering that's being done on you.

Browser Extension: HTTPS Everywhere
https://www.eff.org/https-everywhere
If I can't sell you on using Tor, the least you can do is install this great web browser extension which will help secure the connection between your browser and a lot of websites that are less secure than they should be in 2017. Thankfully, our friends at the EFF have developed the extension HTTPS Everywhere that not only solves that problem, but is quick and easy to install.

Delete Social Media Accounts: Just Delete Me
http://justdeleteme.xyz/
There used to be this great website called "Just Delete Me", which helped you find where to go to delete your information on most popular social media websites and other outlets. The site itself doesn't seem to be updated anymore, but the shell of it is still online at the time of this writing. That shell provides more than enough information to get you started in terms of deleting old accounts or accounts you no longer want to have online.

CHAPTER SUMMARY

➤ In addition to using the tools I mentioned in this chapter, if you are the victim of a data breach like what happened with Equifax, you should make sure to subscribe to a credit monitoring service and keep a close eye on your bank account for any shady activity. You should also directly contact the company that was hacked, to see if there are any other steps you can take to protect yourself. Finally, you should go and update all your passwords. Personally, I keep a notebook offline with all my passwords in it, and when it comes time to change them, I just cross out the old entry and add a new one. It's best to change your passwords at least once a year.

➤ Don't forget that Facebook does let you opt out of some of its tracking over in the Settings tab. Ditto with Twitter. Don't be afraid to explore the settings on your favourite platform or device to see if they offer you a way to limit tracking and further protect your privacy. I think we're at a cultural tipping point where these settings are increasingly expected by consumers and tech companies will have to provide them.

CHAPTER TWO

WWI AND THE LAST DAYS OF PRIVACY

As America entered the First World War, it did so with a wary eye on issues abroad (the rise of Fascism and Communism) and domestic (the waves of immigrants who seemingly didn't want to assimilate). These issues, as well as the war itself, led the government to make a series of decisions that defined privacy for its citizens, and citizens of countries around the world, forever.

For most Americans, the government collecting data en masse, and doing who-knows-what with it, is less than desirable. But government data collection has been happening for over one hundred years. There seem to be specific moments, historically speaking, where the public gets worked up about its government eavesdropping. Then we forget about it, and data collection continues until someone else reminds us that it's happening. This enrages the public all over again, until we're lulled back to sleep with iPads filled with episodes of *Fuller House*. We forget that this sort of mass data collection on civilian population has been going on since time immemorial, and so a little reminder now and again that this is happening is a good thing. Here's a quick test to show you what I mean: remember that time when the NSA was passing around sexy photos of people that they came across in their data collection efforts? No. Well, that was only a few years ago. How quickly we forget...

So, I don't see much of a point in wasting your time talking about what the American government (or any government for that matter) does on the data collection front. They've been doing it forever, and will continue to do it long after all that's left on this Earth are Ryan Seacrest and his larvae. The only point I'm making here is reminding you how mass data collection and surveillance got started.

It's important to understand when the relationship between the American government and its citizens changed to where mass data collection was deemed necessary. Because, what stems from that change, I argue, is the end of privacy. It was during this time that the government started collecting data and asking private companies to share their data with them. Other countries followed suit, because if Americans could get away with doing this, why not them? As technology became more sophisticated, so did the ability of the state and private companies to obtain even more data. And since those companies and the government, were sharing all that data anyway some had the bright idea to start making a profit from it. Everything that we'll talk about in this book had a very specific starting point, and that point is World War I.

Don't trust those Germans!

If you're an American, World War I is usually a blip on the radar screen of history class. This is because America didn't get involved in the global conflict until almost the end of the war, and also because most history teachers are stuck teaching to tests generated by large for-profit companies that have swindled their way into completely dominating the American education system. So, if it's not the Pilgrims, the Revolution, the Civil War, or World War II, odds are most kids aren't going to learn about it, because it won't be on the test. Given this trend, it's not surprising that we don't stop to think about 'the war to end all wars' anymore, aside from maybe marvelling at how badass Gal Gadot's Wonder Woman looked fighting her way across No Man's Land in the movie. (She did indeed look pretty badass.)

Although the United States didn't join WWI until it was almost over, people in America took sides from the very beginning. Some went to other countries, like France or Canada, in order to fight against the Germans. There were also reports of German Americans, and recent immigrants to America from Germany, who left the US to fight for Germany. Then there were reports that Germany had thousands of men, already in America, who were going to take part in an invasion of Canada in order to force the British to split their focus between two fronts. As entering the war looked more and more likely, pervasive anti-German sentiment finally became such an issue that presidential candidates were weighing in on whether any German Americans could be trusted. Entering the war itself was also an election issue, with Woodrow Wilson running for a second term as president with the slogan "He kept us out of war!" And when America finally entered the war, not long after Wilson was re-elected president, Wilson decided to do a series of things that changed the fabric of the country. This included the passage of the Espionage Act, which you may have seen in the news during the NSA/Snowden standoff. That's the law Snowden would be tried under if he ever returns to America. Hopefully he hasn't come back by the time you read this, making this section horribly out of date. I personally hope he stays overseas and continues to be like our own Punxsutawney Phil who randomly appears to warn us about the government being creepy, before vanishing again.

Anyway, concerns about spies in America date back to 1798 and the Alien Enemies Act, which allowed for the government to arrest and seize the property of citizens of other countries residing in the US. However, Wilson's actions following entry into WWI in 1917 were without precedent. First, some German Americans were rounded up and placed in internment camps, while others were forced to register with the government as part of the government's effort to track their movements and whereabouts during the conflict. Then, Wilson and Congress passed the Espionage Act.

Wilson's Espionage Act made it illegal for US citizens to aid 'the enemy' (whoever that might be at any given moment) by providing 'the enemy' with information concerning America's activity, or by misleading our country about 'the enemy's' activity. Check out what Wilson said in 1915 when he first proposed the act:

"There are citizens of the United States, I blush to admit, born under other flags but welcomed under our generous naturalization laws to the full freedom and opportunity of America, who have poured the poison of disloyalty into the very arteries of our national life; who have sought to bring the authority and good name of our Government into contempt, to destroy our industries wherever they thought it effective for their vindictive purposes to strike at them, and to debase our politics to the uses of foreign intrigue."

Sound familiar? It's the exact same rationale that was used to justify the passage of the USA Patriot Act in 2001, nearly a hundred years later, and the ascension to presidency of Donald Trump in 2016. Both the Espionage Act and the Patriot Act came after acts of war and terrorism against American citizens. Months before Woodrow Wilson gave his speech, the RMS *Lusitania* had been sunk by German U-boats, leading to the deaths of nearly 1,200 people, including 128 Americans.

To assimilate or not to assimilate...

You can see, then, the rationale for what comes next. Back in 1915, and leading into the American war effort in 1917, much like today, there were abundant amounts of fear, paranoia, and misinformation floating around, in addition to real and credible threats. The United States, as a federal government, had never really experienced that sort of paranoia prior to the explosion of immigration into the country in the 1880s. In the 1880s and throughout most of the twentieth century, there was an entire generation of people born in the United States encountering people who were coming here from Western and Eastern Europe and bringing their cultures along with them. It was, for example, around this time that we saw an influx of Jews coming to America, including my Grandmother and Grandfather's family on both sides.

Unlike other immigration streams into America prior to the 1880s, the sheer number and density of this wave allowed people from different backgrounds to come and settle down among people just like themselves, meaning there was less desire to assimilate—and then, assimilate with what? There was no prevailing identity as such, just a patchwork of disparate ethnic, religious, cultural, linguistic backgrounds. Now, throw in a fear of communism, war, as well as good ol'-fashioned prejudice, and you can see how the government did what it did.

The same period also marked the beginnings of a global communications network, which allowed for better and faster communication between the Old World and the New World—often to the detriment of both, thanks to things like the beginnings of propaganda campaigns and yellow journalism, or what we today refer to as 'Fake News'. This convergence of paranoia and technology gave way to the erosion of citizens' privacy by the government and communications companies. During WWI, the American government, supported by the Espionage Act, decided to begin taking measures to protect itself. But when the war ended, the government was still feeling unsure. Little could they predict that if they had just waited a couple of generations, everyone in my family would be speaking English and refusing to go to temple because there were better things to do, like catch a Mets game. Assimilation, it seems, was round the corner.

An extreme willingness to help

The government pays a visit to the president of Western Union, who is described as being "anxious to do everything he could [to help the government]". One hundred years later, AT&T is described as having "an extreme willingness to help" the NSA. Not much has changed. The technology certainly has, but the willingness of corporations to hand over the data they have on you to the government has not. And don't let Google, Facebook, Microsoft, Amazon, and Apple fool you with their public protests. They're just as eager to help the government, provided the government looks the other way on their FTC and DOJ investigations. (For more on that duplicitous behaviour, I highly recommend you watch the 2013 documentary *Terms and Conditions May Apply*). And, speaking of Facebook, since 2011 they've lobbied the Federal Election Commission to be exempt from rules and regulations that would have forced them to be transparent concerning the purchase of political advertising. In other words, like with television or radio, if someone bought political ads on Facebook, they would have been compelled to tell you and the government who purchased those advertisements and allow the advertisements to be viewable by all.

This is crucial because, until around the time I

finished this book, there was a common practice on Facebook called 'Dark Advertising'. If I were to run a dark advertisement, that advertisement wouldn't run on my official Facebook Page, Facebook.com/BJMendelson. Instead, only people I targeted with the advertisement would be able to see it. That gives me deniability: I could say I never ran an ad because not everyone could see it or prove where it came from. And, more commonly, I can decide to only show that ad to people who would agree with it, thus reinforcing their beliefs. This is something that later would come back and haunt Facebook, namely the purchase of advertisements in swing states during the 2016 presidential election by Russian operators, and the company's failure to disclose who purchased those ads in the first place. Whoops.

The relationship between the US government and US communications companies, where the government gains access to networks controlled by these companies (be they telegraph operators or ISPs) in order to snoop on citizens via their private data and communications, has gone through some stops and starts that we continue to see today. I mentioned there are these brief moments when we get mad about what the government does, and the government temporarily stops before starting up again after we forget what they're doing. This pattern has been fairly consistent since World War I. In that time, we've seen the government ally with private communications companies to harvest your data in the name of searching for, and stopping, crises before they start. Whether they're successful is debatable. The recent shooting in Las Vegas, and the Boston Marathon bombing prove that most government data collection isn't worth a damn when it comes to preventing such events, but that's just what I think. However, the effectiveness of that mass data collection is not quite the point here. The point is, government snooping isn't new and it certainly didn't start with the aftermath of 9/11, or thanks to Google.

CHAPTER SUMMARY

➢ The federal government has been collecting massive amounts of data on its citizens since World War I. They have been aided by for-profit companies like Western Union and AT&T.

➢ The justification for the data collection was the idea that America had enemies disguised as regular citizens among its growing immigration population. If this rationale sounds familiar, it's because we are still hearing it over one hundred years later. Few things sell better than fear.

➢ There's a seemingly endless cycle throughout American history of citizens getting pissed off about the government's invasion of privacy and collection of data, which tends to lead to the government temporarily backing off on these practices. They then resume the same practices when citizens go back to being distracted and forget about what it was they were so mad about in the first place. Take note of this pattern.

➢ Tech companies, especially in recent memory, may publicly protest the government asking them for data, but the truth is they're (usually) very forthcoming with the government when asked.

CHAPTER THREE

REGULATION IS BULLSHIT!

Do you know who Glenn Greenwald is? He's an American journalist and founder of *The Intercept*. You might know him from his time contributing to *The Guardian*, but it's okay if you don't. Neither did I. What brought Greenwald to international attention was the incident involving Edward Snowden, a Booz Allen Hamilton contractor assigned to the NSA. Snowden shared with Greenwald documents from the NSA that detailed the organization's comprehensive system for spying on Americans. Before we talk about that, here's why you might not know who Greenwald or Snowden are: we tend to forget about things that don't have ramifications on our day-to-day lives. In the first Sherlock Holmes story, *A Study in Scarlet*, Holmes admonishes Watson for telling him that the Earth revolves around the sun—the opposite of what Holmes believed. Holmes didn't care what the truth was. The fact that the Earth revolves around the Sun was irrelevant to his day-to-day life, and as far as the detective was concerned, this useless information would make it harder for him to access more important things in his mind when he needed them. We're a lot like Sherlock: if it doesn't affect us in a noticeable way, who cares?

We should care, but don't

This attitude makes any privacy discussion difficult to have without people's eyes glazing over or getting the riposte "I have nothing to hide!" You totally do, by the way, have something to hide. Otherwise you'd give me your email password without hesitation and let me follow you into the bathroom. We all have something to hide. Even if it's a secret love for the worst video game film ever made, 1994's *Double Dragon*. It's fine. But let's just all agree that the 'I have nothing to hide' argument in any privacy discussion needs to be kicked into a volcano somewhere and take its rightful place among the ashes. You either care, or you don't because you're getting free entertainment in exchange for your data. Although…

This is a short tangent, but it's an important one. There's no such thing as 'free'. So, if Spotify is giving you free music in exchange for running targeted advertisements on you based on your data, that's a great arrangement for you and Spotify. But this arrangement sucks for artists because it devalues their music. People come to expect that music should cost them nothing, or close to nothing. That in turn means fewer people are able to pursue a career as musicians.

By extension, it renders music an easy target for public school 'reformers', who then cut arts funding because they think science, technology, engineering, and maths (STEM) is the way of the future. But it's the other way around. When automation really kicks in over the next ten to twenty years for our society, the people flipping burgers are going to be the STEM majors whose technical prowess can easily be replicated by machines. Anyway, the point here is, 'free' isn't actually free. Someone is losing on that transaction. It might be the musicians or the music industry, or it could be you and your privacy. As Jaron Lanier points out, the music might be free, but it's no coincidence your smartphone bill keeps going up as well. Their music might be free for you, but if the musician's only source of income is from touring constantly, what happens when they get sick or have other obligations that prevent them from doing so?

Of course, we're all concerned about who is accessing our data and what they're doing with it, but we also don't care that much. That's the twist. Not in the sense of doing something about it anyway. Data from the Pew Research Center supports this notion. (Pew is a nonpartisan think tank that produces a lot of studies about the habits of Americans, particularly when it comes to demographic trends. They're fairly reliable, and the odds are good that most media outlets that you enjoy rely on them heavily.) A Pew study confirmed what I'm saying here by showing that an overwhelming majority of Americans care about their privacy and who has access to their data but, at the same time, an overwhelming majority of Americans have no confidence in their data remaining private. Fewer still take actions to protect their data.

If someone's going to profit off your personal information, it might as well be you. Your data. Your choice. I'm not the only one who thinks so, as this idea was at the core of Lanier's book *Who Owns the Future?* For all their talk about a universal basic income, the tech titans don't seem to be forthcoming about ways for the government to pay for such a thing. I have what I think is a brilliant (if not original) suggestion, that Facebook and friends pay you an annual salary in exchange for collecting and selling your data to advertisers and other parties—if they don't like the idea of advertisers paying you directly for a little bit of your attention, that is. How's that for fair?

I mention state governments throughout this book because I have no confidence in the federal government's ability to get anything done anymore. But thankfully, elsewhere in the world, governments are doing great things to protect data and privacy. Great things. Terrific things. The best things…(sighs deeply). Anyway, that means that we actually have legal and regulatory templates to follow here in the States if we can't get the tech companies to regulate themselves, or let an independent party do it for them. The European Union has rules that are called the General Data Protection Regulation (GDPR), which protect the online privacy of citizens of the Union. (The United Kingdom is following this regulation and will have their own on the books once they've separated from the EU as well.) The American government has nothing like GDPR, despite numerous attempts by privacy groups and at least one president (the only good one of the twenty-first century) to change that. And it boils down to lobbying. Alphabet (the company formerly known as Google) is one of the top companies in the United States spending money on … you guessed it, lobbying. According to OpenSecrets.org, 78 out of 92 lobbyists that Alphabet paid in 2015–2016 used to work for the federal government. Facebook spent just over eight million dollars on lobbying in 2016, and associated groups lobbying on behalf of Facebook spent $1,010,000. Of the lobbyists that worked on behalf of Facebook in 2016, OpenSecrets reports that 93 percent of them used to hold government positions before joining Facebook or working on their behalf. This includes one former Republican congressman from Arizona, John Shadegg. Apple has spent $4.6 million on lobbying the federal government so far in 2017, with 38 out of 42 lobbyists having worked for the government before taking a job with them, as reported by OpenSecrets. I could go on, but you get the point here. The American tech companies don't want the government involved in their business, but at the same time, they're happy to hand over all the data they have on you to the government when asked. And, if you really want to get mad, look up how much money Amazon, Google, Facebook, Microsoft, Apple, and their friends have either outright refused to pay in taxes or have got around paying by abusing the system. We're talking billions of dollars here that could be going back into public schools to keep things like art and music from being cut in the first place. We would not be having the national debate we're currently having over infrastructure, education funding, and health care if these companies just paid taxes.

By giving control over the data back to users—and making companies that want to collect that data do so more explicitly—the consequences of a GDPR-like law in the United States would be devastating for US-based companies like Alphabet, Microsoft, Apple, Amazon, and Facebook. For one thing, if a company suffers a data breach in the EU, that company would be subject to some pretty heavy financial fines under GDPR. But, more importantly, GDPR provides EU consumers with a clearer understanding of what is being done with their data, the ability to request that data, and the ability to use a service even if they opt out of that data collection. There's already been at least one instance where a European journalist requested data from the popular dating app Tinder to see what information the company is collecting about users. Since Tinder is based in the United States, it didn't necessarily have to comply (they didn't tell the journalist her desirability score, for example, which is how their system ranks you in relation to potential matches). But the journalist, Judith Duportail, got more than she expected when she received over 800 pages of information Tinder had collected on her. This included every conversation she had ever had on Tinder along with other information she had supplied (jobs, likes, taste in men), and some things she hadn't (her Facebook friends and Facebook likes). In her breakdown of the data received, Judith also noted in her piece for *The Guardian* that Tinder's privacy policy (the thing no one reads) says explicitly that the data they collect on you can be used for advertising purposes. Under GDPR, if Judith or other Tinder users in the EU withdraw their consent for Tinder to use their data, the company must then delete all the data it has on them. The data can also be deleted at a user's request if it's been involved in a security breach, or if the data is no longer necessary.

Cool, right? Not for the tech companies. Tinder is out of all that potential advertising revenue it could have made. This is great for you and me, but for the tech company, not so much. If we had similar laws in the US, that would mean I could ask Facebook, Google, or any other platform to delete my data if it was no longer being used after a certain period of time, and I could also withdraw my consent for them to use that data at any time (and they'd have to delete it if I did). This is why I'm a fan of the idea of getting an ad-free option for sites like Facebook or Instagram. I don't mind paying a few dollars for access to these platforms if it means they're not serving me advertisements and selling my data to other people. I'd also love additional features, but I know I'm in the minority on this front.

Not that the tech companies want to give you that option. The algorithms and processes we use to make big data useful only work proportionately to the volume of information that can be collected. So, restricting the immense flow of data could cripple that part of the tech business that depends on gobbling up as much info as they can. And then, to throw a further wrench into their works, if that river of data starts to dry up, the tech companies would have less to sell to advertisers. This makes their data less valuable to brands and other advertisers, since there would be fewer people to target, and with less accuracy, than if they had as much data as they could collect. The less data available, the less accurate and useful the service. The less data collected, the less valuable these platforms are to advertisers. And then, when you factor in concerns that brands and advertisers have involving brand safety, it definitely calls into question whether further investment in these digital marketing channels would be worth it. Let me ask you something: who in their right mind thinks six seconds' worth of anything is enough to advertise to someone outside of Google and their friends? Yet here we are, dumping money into Snapchat, Facebook, and other platforms that offer exactly that, or less.

So, while the European Union and other countries are well on their way to addressing the problems discussed here, the American government is woefully behind.

Unintended consequences

Some of this mess, to be fair, is not intentional. Laws can't keep up with the pace of innovation. The Fair Credit Reporting Act provides you with some protection concerning the potential use of social media and other data to determine your credit score. But it doesn't protect you from other parties like your bank, landlord, or prospective employers scooping up that data to render a decision about you. That's nobody's fault, provided we take measures to correct this issue immediately. If the laws on the books suck, then it doesn't matter where in the world you are. Until your country cracks the whip, you'd better believe the creepy stuff that tech and other companies pull around the world is also going to be pulled on you.

I care about what the government can do to protect the people from these companies, in the same way they used to protect people from Standard Oil and Microsoft. My fellow children of the 1990s will remember that Microsoft was the dominant power in tech before they started making awesome video game consoles. A Department of Justice investigation and lawsuit helped put a stop to the nightmare of Internet Explorer and its global reign of terror. So, if we were able to do that twenty years ago, we most certainly can do the same now to Google, Facebook, Amazon, and Apple. These companies will tell you that any sort of regulation will stop or hinder their innovation, but these are the same people who want to convince you that algorithms are magic and no one can understand what they do aside from computer scientists and other people in Silicon Valley who don't know how to interact with women or hire a diverse workforce. Don't believe them. It's nonsense, intended to keep people from examining how a lot of tech companies actually work. An algorithm is just as frightening as Tracy Jordan's *Werewolf Bar Mitzvah* video. Algorithms are no different than the recipes your grandmother used to make brownies. It's a set of instructions. That's it. I enjoy using OkCupid, but I know their match score is bullshit based on garbage data. We only go by the match score because we think this stuff is magic and computers know better than us. They don't. They know what we tell them. Never forget that.

For example, if you go to Barnes & Noble and buy a whole bunch of *Sailor Moon* manga, Barnes & Noble's system will tell them to give you a coupon on manga and even predict your next purchase. That's awesome, but the system has no idea why you're buying manga in the first place. Big Data doesn't know why you do what you do, it just knows that you did it. You could, for example, have a sick relative in the hospital who loves *Sailor Moon* and you wanted to give them something to read while they recover.

That means that if you suddenly stop buying *Sailor Moon* items, Barnes & Noble has no idea why. I mention this because some people may argue that the government and companies need all the data they can get in order to better predict things and provide better services as mentioned above, but the reality is that big data can also be really daft.

CHAPTER SUMMARY

➢ There's not much we can do about the federal government spying on us, but there's plenty we can do on the state level to tighten up the laws, rules, and other regulations to make it harder for for-profit enterprises to invade our privacy and make a profit from it.

➢ For those of you who don't like the idea of any sort of government regulation, there are tools out there you can use to help protect some of your data. As time goes by, there may also be some private-industry solutions that bubble up to help mitigate the problem of companies invading your privacy to make some money off you. For example, there's a lot of talk of using the private ledger functionality found within cryptocurrencies like Bitcoin to allow people to have total control over their own data. Up to and including having the ability to sell it to companies like Facebook, Google, Amazon, Apple, and Microsoft.

➢ One other thing I'd like to see: data literacy being taught in high school and worked into the curriculum.

CHAPTER FOUR

BIG TROUBLE IN LITTLE DATA

'Big data.' 'Metadata.' 'Raw data.' Data processed by autonomous machines employing 'machine learning'. By the time you read this, there will be more data-related buzzwords than I can possibly list, especially relating to the use of your data by artificial intelligence. Since this is not a book on AI, we won't get into that topic here, but I will share with you this: there's a running joke in the artificial intelligence industry that anything that hasn't been invented yet is referred to as AI. Everything else that actually develops from that field, like machine learning (which does involve your data and privacy) has its own name, and in some cases, the technology behind it is many decades old. Where machine learning is concerned, the thing to keep in the back of your mind is that the information we're entering into Google, Amazon, Facebook, and other platforms is being used to make better recipes (algorithms) with more data. So, in yet another instance where 'free' isn't necessarily free, the smarter we make those systems, the more likely we are to further the speed of automation—and that means fewer jobs and opportunities for our fellow humans.

That aside, the thing to underline here is that your data is incredibly valuable when it comes to non-government entities. Period. Full stop. Because of this, your privacy has the potential to be violated in a number of ways, by multiple parties, in order to serve various private interests. This will increasingly involve things like machine learning. And we're not just talking about data collected from your smartphones, smartwatches, and laptops. If you use a voice-activated assistant like a Google Assistant or Amazon Alexa, or if you're reading this inside an autonomous vehicle, there are some major issues surrounding your data involving those respective products as well. Amazon's new Alexa Spot basically puts a camera in your bedroom. A lot of self-driving car software systems keep track of everywhere you go in order to make the best recommendations about how you can get there in the future. But the fact that you keep going to that one Adam & Eve's location in Columbus also gets picked up. Those visits get shared with other parties by the software powering your self-driving car—other parties who may start sending you targeted messaging about coupons and deals you can use at Adam & Eve on *Wonder Woman* costumes for your significant other to wear in the bedroom.

There's often a lot of confusion about the kind of data being collected by these companies through their sites, devices, and apps. What I'd like to do here, then, is explain the different types of data these companies are collecting about you, and then discuss what makes them valuable in the first place. Just a note: what data is, and how it's collected, changes often. So consider the information below to be a good starting point for discussions on privacy, but not the last word.

Disparate data

In recent years, the Federal Trade Commission (FTC) has pushed Congress to force the businesses behind many apps and Internet-enabled platforms to be more clear and honest about the type of data they're collecting from their users.

The FTC breaks that data down into twelve unique groups:

1. Identifying data (your name, address, phone numbers, and emails).

2. Sensitive Identifying data (your Social Security Number, Driver's License number, and birthday).

3. Demographic data (your height, race, religion, and marital status).

4. Court and Public Records data (bankruptcies, judgements, liens, and your political party affiliation).

5. Social Media and Technology data (your platform of choice and how much you use it, how many 'friends' you are connected with, your Internet Service Provider, and how much you use the Internet).

6. Home and Neighbourhood data (how much you pay in rent, how much you pay on your mortgage, the value of your home).

7. General Interest data (how much gambling you might do, the type of clothes you like to buy, the shows you

watch, the kind of pets you own).

8. Vehicle data (whether you own a car, what car you own, your car preference, and your car-buying habits — and with autonomous vehicles you can expect this category to expand greatly in the next decades).

9. Financial data (your credit, the loans you have, the type of credit cards you may own).

10. Travel data (your preferred hotel, your preferred airline, the kind of vacations you take).

11. Purchase Behaviour data (how much you spend, the type of things you buy, and your preference in terms of how and where you buy your stuff).

12. Health data (your prescriptions, whether you have allergies, whether you wear glasses; in other words, the kind of things only your doctors should know).

Mo data mo problems

Everything in this book, and most of the debate concerning privacy not pertaining to the government, rests on one key fact: your data is worth a fortune, and every day, regardless of what Internet-enabled device you choose to use, you create more and more of it for someone else to profit from. Did you pick up your phone first thing in the morning to text your sex kitten using iMessage? You created more data. Did you ask Alexa what the weather is like this morning? You created more data. Did you send some emails? Data. Did your self-driving car take you somewhere? Data. Did you use Google Maps on your phone to find that famous sex dungeon in Los Angeles? More data created. Did your Apple

Watch congratulate you on how many times you stood up today? Data. Did you visit Pornhub at least twice today to see if anyone uploaded any new superheroine porn? Even more data created. Have I mentioned yet that Facebook has the largest data set of faces in the world and doesn't even need to see your face at this point to identify you in pictures that get uploaded to their system? Yeah, they totally do. All with the goal of selling that information to advertisers so they can target you based on your emotions. Remember that the next time you're feeling sad and Facebook starts serving you nothing but Ben & Jerry's ads. The list goes on, but I think you're getting the picture. If you do something with an Internet-enabled device, you're creating valuable data that everyone wants a piece of. (Whether the data is worth a damn for advertising purposes is a different story entirely, and really irrelevant after a certain point, because you can't suddenly stand up and go "all of this is bullshit" and expect multiple multibillion-dollar industries to change their policies and actions all at once. Believe me... I tried.)

Your data makes money for data brokers and data providers like Acxiom, Datalogix, Epsilon, Experian, Equifax, Oracle, WPP, and TransUnion. The Fair Credit Reporting Act only protects you from three of those companies, by the way, and most of this data is passed around without first being encrypted, making your data easy to find and way less secure than it should be on these servers.

Facebook purchases data from these and other companies in order to recommend products and run advertisements in your feed, as well as make other suggestions. Facebook then turns around to large companies, some of whom now have Facebook and Google employees within their marketing ranks, to sell them on investing more money into Google and Facebook's platforms because of how well they can target you. WPP is the world's largest advertising holding company and there is a revolving door between them and Facebook and Google. As NYU Professor Scott Galloway points out, there have been around 2,000 employees of WPP thus far that have migrated to Facebook and Google.

Advertisers and other parties can also upload the emails they purchase from these companies and then specifically target you on platforms like Facebook. This is what the Russian operatives did in battleground states during the 2016 US presidential election, after allegedly breaking into voter registration systems operated by a company called VR Systems.

These data brokers and data providers also funnel data from websites, apps, and smart devices (with and without your knowledge) to build a profile on you that they can sell. So yes, your paranoid friend who thought the CIA was talking to them through their microwave was right. Someone does indeed have a file on you with all your information. It's just not necessarily the government. And if that file were to get out, if it includes data like your browsing history, you could be in for some trouble. That's why I never bought the "I have nothing to hide" argument. You mean to tell me there's nothing in your browsing history that couldn't embarrass you or cause you to lose your job if your boss saw it? Really? Even I clean out my browser history regularly, and everyone reading this book now knows I have a superheroine-in-peril fetish.

Your data creates market opportunities for tech companies looking for ad dollars in exchange for selling aggregate profiles of their users. Your data is worth something to numerous, numerous parties. If it wasn't so, it's likely that most of our concerns regarding privacy addressed in this book wouldn't be so pressing because no one would want our data in the first place. It's one thing to tell people, "If you use something for free on the Internet, you are the product", but it's quite another to tell them that their personal data is worth a fortune and others are getting rich from it. And, as I've said, and hopefully at this point you agree, I'm a big believer that you should be getting a cut of the action if someone is making money off your stuff. Same goes for any other membership or loyalty program out there. And I'm not letting your local grocery store off the hook, either. There are plenty of ways to get rich in America, but being creepy doesn't have to be one of them.

The company that creeps

Before we go any further, I'd like to say something about 'being creepy.' 'Creepy' refers specifically to unethical behaviour, not illegal behaviour. The issues today involving the use and abuse of your data are the result of a lack of sufficient law and oversight meant to protect it, a lack of education on the part of the public when it comes to protecting itself, and knowing about the kind of data being collected about it in the first place. We're over a third of the way through this book and I haven't even gotten to the fact that the overwhelming majority of people my age (and younger) in the United States are all walking around with microphones and tracking devices in our pockets in the form of our smartphones. Devices where the engineers and company may tell you that your favourite app isn't using your phone's microphone to listen to your conversation, but it is. (This includes your Amazon Echoes and Google Assistants too.) While there is a major economic incentive to scoop up all this data in ethical and unethical ways, if there were better laws and oversight by the government or an independent party, a lot of the unethical behaviour would be curtailed. So while 'creepy' in this book doesn't refer to something that is strictly speaking illegal, it does relate to unethical tactics and methods used to collect your data by these companies and other parties.

A quick example: some years back, *The Wall Street Journal* reported that Nielsen—the company best known for producing sketchy data that often leads to your favourite television shows like *Pan Am* and *Son of Zorn* being cancelled—broke into a private online forum and stole what was posted there. Nielsen was working with drug manufacturers, and the forum happened to be for people with emotional disorders to discuss treatments and other ways of taking care of themselves. Nielsen wanted that data in order to give it to the drug companies. You can imagine the horror the users of that forum felt, having their personal stories with their names attached to them, collected from a place they thought was private and secure, and provided to drug companies. Was it illegal? No. Was it creepy? You bet. But here's the kicker: the site Nielsen broke into, PatientsLikeMe.com, had already been selling user information, albeit in a more 'anonymous' form, to interested parties. Pro tip: little is anonymous anymore on the Internet. It is way too easy to identify people with just the tiniest amount of effort. So, when you hear about 'anonymized data' being passed around that doesn't identify anyone, don't believe it. It's bullshit also. Few of us online or offline are truly anonymous. Here's a great example of what I mean: German reporter Svea Eckert was able to get access to the web browsing history of high-profile officials in Germany. Although that information started out as anonymous, with a few short steps, Eckert and the researchers she was working with were able to pin the browsing data to specific people. They were able to connect the information they had with information that was freely and publicly available about those individuals. You might be wondering where the browsing data came from in the first place. Wouldn't you know it, the browser data came from the extensions those people, and many others, had installed in their browsers. One of the methods the researchers had figured out to tie the identity of each person to the browser data that they had was by looking for the locations from which those users had logged into their social media accounts, which often readily revealed their identity.

By the way, installing malware or something like a fake browser extension for Chrome or your favourite browser is something that happens a lot. A fake extension for AdBlock Plus slimed its way into Google's store and infected over 37,000 computers just as I finished working on this manuscript. So, don't start thinking that only suckers fall victim to this kind of stuff.

Even when you think your data is private while using an Internet-enabled device or app, it most likely is not. Your default assumption should always be that if something is free to use, then the price you pay is giving up your privacy. You should also assume that anything connected to the Internet is collecting and sharing data on you, and could be used to spy on you. I know it sounds crazy. But even children's toymaker Mattel almost got in on the act with Aristotle, an announced (and then cancelled) toy that would watch over your baby and comfort them with white noise or a lullaby depending on what the device detected. You know what's hilarious? (This is a tangent, but I think an important one.) If you say the word 'children', you can bet the ears of every politician in shouting distance will start to burn. Mattel's Aristotle was greeted by a letter from a Democrat and a Republican senator asking Mattel how the information recorded and stored by Aristotle would be used, and who it would be shared with. It's wonderful that they were asking such questions, don't get me wrong, but where were these two senators, and the rest of the federal government, while everything else I talk about in this book was going down?

For a number of years, I used the service Unroll.Me. It was a simple tool that helped clean up my inbox and manage my email subscriptions. When you work in the marketing industry, part of your job is to try not to drown every day in the deluge of newsletters, updates, and other industry drivel you have to read to stay current with your peers. Unroll.Me didn't cost anything to use. It was free.

I should have known better, but like most people I didn't, and as it turns out, Unroll.Me was selling my information to other companies like Uber. Since Unroll.Me scans everyone's email inbox as part of the process of filtering out spam and dumb newsletters, it also knows everything you have coming in, like Uber or Lyft receipts. Uber purchased the data from Unroll.Me's parent company to gauge, in an allegedly anonymous fashion, how well their competitor was doing. As I'll repeat a lot in this book: anonymized data is a bullshit concept. Any expectation of privacy goes out the window the second you use that 'free' platform, or bring an Internet-enabled device into your home. Because the truth is, even if you knowingly agree to give away some of your data in exchange for using the platform, that doesn't stop the company behind the platform from later revising their Terms of Service to get more of it. Which is the real shame here, because I bet most people would be copacetic with giving up some of their information in order to use a free service—as long as they were explicitly and openly doing so. That's another reason why it's so hard to get people to care about the issue of privacy in the first place. Most people live quiet, somewhat boring lives where they're not bothering anyone and don't have any crazy political views, if they have any political views at all. Did you ever wonder why American voter turnout is almost always at the bottom in comparison to other developed countries that have open elections?

And so the data collection thing doesn't even register as an issue. The idea that people are also going to become proactive in telling companies what they can and can't do isn't going to fly. A lot of you taking the time to read this will make the necessary changes to protect yourself, and maybe even advocate for better regulation (through the government or otherwise) of the companies utilizing our data—but there's a whole lot of people who won't.

These folks, like me, enjoy using Google and Facebook and appreciate the convenience and custom tailoring that can be brought about in their user experience thanks to some of the data collection described in this book. To a point, that is. And a lot of those people have enough things going on in their lives to preoccupy them. I have two mentally disabled brothers. My Dad takes care of them. One of those brothers has lately been on a fit of destruction throughout the house, thus far victimizing two sets of blinds, a chair, the shower faucet, and a drawer in the kitchen that looks like it was kicked in by the Incredible Hulk. Do you think my Dad has the time to read *Moby Dick*-length Terms of Service agreements and go into the settings of his platform or browser or Internet-enabled device? No! And he shouldn't have to! It's not our responsibility, nor should it be. So let's be fair here. People shouldn't be forced to jump through unnecessary hoops just so a bunch of tech and advertising companies can't take advantage of them.

Asking people to worry about their privacy and about what's being done with all that personal data that's collected to give them a nice experience (on top of worrying about everything else in their lives) is asking more than you'd think. Putting aside the Internet-enabled devices you own or find yourself around (don't forget, even if you don't have a smartphone, your friend sure does), there are hundreds of sensors and cameras out there right now taking pictures and readings of your data. And every year, those sensors and cameras get increasingly more sophisticated, collecting even more data. When exactly did you get a say about that? You didn't. The ubiquity of these sensors is at the point where crimes are actively being sold by collecting data from them. Who owns that data? Where's it all going?

But let's just focus on protecting your privacy online, because that is a never-ending battle in itself. It's one thing that can be addressed, despite often being a pain, involving the finding of the right solution for the right problem and finding ways to plug the holes when those solutions don't cover everything. Then you have to factor in keeping that software up to date, and then what do you do when someone compromises it and you have to start all over again? I know. It sounds like I'm making excuses for lazy people, but I encourage you not to think that. We all have things to do, and most people work hard jobs that keep them busy all day and provide them with little time to do much of anything else beyond take care of their kids (if they have any) and themselves. Now you want to ask them to remain in a state of constant vigilance because of a bunch of greedy corporations? It's a tough sell. The government has to get involved, the corporations should be paying those people for using their data in any way beyond providing them with the free service they enjoy, and those customers should be given way more control over what data is being collected, and for how long. In this way, if the customer wants to take a few minutes to opt out of the tracking, or have their data erased, they can do so. This is not a hard problem to solve; it just takes a healthy acceptance of reality, and an understanding that things often don't work as well as they look on paper when applied to real life. I don't want to do a lot of moralizing and philosophizing, but I do think we have an obligation to the people around us to look out for them the best way we can. Yes, that's a good place to start.

CHAPTER SUMMARY

➢ People are busy. Tech companies are lying to you. Your data is not safe no matter what anyone tells you. You can do something about this, and help other people in the process, or you can continue doing what you're doing. Your call.

CHAPTER FIVE

THE SOCIAL MEDIA INDUSTRIAL COMPLEX

Nine times out of ten, nobody is given any sort of explicit control over who has their data and what's being done with it. You might be able to flip a switch or two within Facebook or Twitter's settings, but that doesn't even begin to slow down the amount of data they're grabbing about you. Aside from altering the Terms of Service at any time they choose, the platforms and companies also may not inform you that the use of their app also means that your data will be shared with a data broker like Acxiom. Or, as is incredibly common in the name of 'growth hacking', that the platform or app will quietly upload all of your contacts from your phone's address book, spam them, and then collect all your friends' information in addition to yours. LinkedIn settled out of court to the tune of $13 million for spamming people you were connected to in your address book. Both MySpace and Facebook spammed people in their early days to quickly grow their user base, with Facebook notably spamming everyone at Harvard. Underneath most of the stories about 'viral' phenomena or 'red hot' start-ups, you'll often find something creepy being done to grow rapidly, and that almost always involves abusing your data.

Why is your data worth so much in the first place? Let's look at that argument another way. The value of your data is rooted in a questionable belief that Internet-based data collection companies can provide better and more precise data about consumers than traditional media outlets, and thus can better target consumers on behalf of big brands and advertising agencies. Not everyone believes targeted Internet advertising is all it's cracked up to be. I sure don't, but enough people do to the point where there's big money to be made in scooping up and selling data to brands and large companies. Don't take my word for it, though: Google was running ads on PolitiFact, a fact-checking website, promoting fake news websites. You can't make this shit up.

Despite all of that, according to *The Guardian*, Google and Facebook "attracted one-fifth of global advertising spending" in 2016, with Google collecting $79.4 billion and Facebook collecting $26.9 billion. So, if you're wondering how much your data is worth, those numbers should give you a good place to start. This isn't a marketing book, so I won't get too much into how stupid it is to flush money down the toilet on micro-targeting people using this data. But I will say that your data would be way less valuable if tech companies hadn't succeeded in brainwashing brands and ad agencies about how great and useful their platforms are for doing just that over the past twenty years. The funny thing is that if you explicitly provide your data to a company, or they pay you for the right to advertise to you, that's infinitely more valuable than anything Google, Facebook, and Amazon are currently serving up to their customers. At least there you're actually expressing an interest, as opposed to some algorithm of questionable intelligence just assuming you're into something because of the data it collected.

What happens, then, with all this data? There are plenty of good, legitimate uses. All those sensors and cameras collecting information on you may sound scary, but that data could be used to fix the New York City Subway system, and to figure out population trends and which areas might need to be protected as sea levels continue to rise. So, just to be clear, in this book we're not going to discuss all the good causes, because I don't have a problem with that, and I bet most of you don't have a problem with that either. Here we're entirely focused on the scummy things being done with your data, often without your knowledge, all in the name of making a quick buck. So, since I mentioned the advertising industry, and because that industry and the tech industry are ground zero for scummy behaviour when it comes to your data, let me give you another example of what happens with all that data collected about you.

One of the challenges of working in the advertising industry is identifying the right audience to target with the right message. Seems obvious, right? We (and I include myself here, because I am currently active as a marketing consultant) want you to buy stuff. So, we have to go where the people are...or where we *think* they are. You see, there's this old adage that is often misquoted by tech people, so-called digital 'gurus', and marketers that goes like this: "Half the money I spend on advertising is wasted; the trouble is, I don't know which half." The thing is, the guy who allegedly said that, John Wanamaker, probably didn't actually say it. It's sort of like how Brutus told everyone he was afraid of zombies in the Bible. That's a funny thing to say to people, but Brutus didn't actually say that, either. In the case of Wanamaker, the truly funny thing is that he — better than many others in his time — knew the power of advertising and how valuable it was in growing prospering business ventures. He didn't need to question whether or not advertising was successful, because he saw the results of it first-hand. Isn't it hilarious that the guy everyone quotes in their argument against advertising was actually successful because of advertising? That's the sort of stupidity we're dealing with when it comes to the justification behind your privacy being abused. And I know I've said this before, but I repeat things because repetition is important in education: the ad and tech industries are really stupid. So, if you're like, "But B.J., if the government was collecting all this data during and after World War I, then why didn't they stop the first terrorist attack on American soil in 1920 by Italian anarchists? Why didn't they stop the Boston Marathon bombing almost one hundred years later in 2013? If we don't know what to do with this data, or have grossly over-inflated its importance and our ability to interpret it, why does every company still want it, and keeps talking about how data is the new oil?" It's because we're not that smart. I wish I had a better answer for you, but I don't. Greedy people do perfectly stupid things in order to make money. Believe me, none of these people are going to turn off the money faucet until the source is completely dried up. If you want an academic explanation, there are plenty of books out there (complete with all the hand-wringing and 'WHAT DOES IT ALL MEAN?' bullshit that authors use to fill pages when they have nothing to say), but I'm not your guy. Your answer is greed. Your second answer is stupidity. And that goes all the way to the top. I was at a conference giving a presentation to government communicators, and someone working on behalf of a very large branch of the government told me that they personally agreed that social media was bullshit, but their bosses were obsessed with it because they were told how magical and wonderful it is. This was in 2017. So, you and I may know this sort of thing is ridiculous, but we're far, far outnumbered by those who don't. Remember: almost 63 million people willingly voted for Donald Trump to be President, and a lot of those people had college degrees.

Because people stupidly believe that advertising using traditional channels like radio, print, and television is wasteful, this allows the tech companies to tell advertising agencies and brands that they've solved that 'waste problem'. How? With all the data they've collected. Since 1994, tech companies have waged extensive, and highly successful, bullshit campaigns to call into question the value of advertising using traditional media, claiming that the Internet and all the data they can collect about you gives them a better way to do it. Over twenty years later, and there's still little proof of that, as you and I know, but good luck trying to convince people otherwise because "a lie told often enough becomes the truth". And so this is what makes your data so valuable. This stupid, vicious cycle of greed and wilful ignorance can only be broken with intervention by the government or an independent group, as well as action on our parts. Or, instead of limiting the data collection completely, at least compensating people directly to get that data straight from the source.

Stupid is as stupid does

The advertising agencies have zero incentive to tell the brands they're wasting their money, and neither do the tech companies. And, since most brands and companies look at marketing as a cost, instead of looking at it as a long-term investment, they are comforted with bullshit numbers like page views and shares because those can be quantified and measured quickly on a spreadsheet. And it also doesn't hurt when you have representatives from Facebook, Twitter, Amazon, and Google walking around your office and telling you what a great idea it is to measure your success off those crooked numbers too. (If I can be a marketing person for a moment, the only other thing you should care about beyond customer lifetime value is whether or not you're making money. Did you see an increase in revenue during the campaign? Great. No metric is perfect, but some metrics don't have $16.4 billion in losses like digital advertising does because of fraud like bots, fake traffic, and embarrassingly low viewability and click-through rates—if those digital ads you pay so much money for even get viewed at all.)

Let me give you one more example from the advertising world that explains what makes your data so valuable. You might be wondering, "why would advertising agencies and others prefer to work with the tech companies, if they have doubts about those online metrics like page views and shares?" I already gave you one answer, complacency, but here's another: because the advertising and marketing worlds are obsessed with things like customer personas, and what better to shape those customer personas than with all the data Facebook, Google, and others say they have at their disposal?

A customer persona looks something like this: 'Sloane' is the name of a customer persona that describes a woman in her twenties who, according to the data collected by Facebook, the agency, and other data brokers, enjoys NPR, likes anime, exercises frequently, and listens to '90s music on her way to work. As far as the data collected is concerned, all of these assumptions are true. (In fact, it's quite easy to dig deep into specific people online on an individual basis these days to confirm that all these things are true, as you saw earlier with the German reporter.) With the data in hand, it is then inferred that not only is the data about Sloane true, but it's also true about all women like Sloane that share similar interests. This is where the wheels fall off the short bus.

How do they 'know' this about the women similar to Sloane? The data shows that this group of people that Sloane is affiliated with on one platform (let's say Facebook) also like NPR. People on other platforms that Sloane frequents all have a higher income and share liberal political tendencies too. Therefore, according to the data, Sloane and women like her listen to NPR, have high incomes and, generally, have liberal political tendencies. Whether or not an actual woman named Sloane even exists, or listens to NPR, etc., is irrelevant to the agency at this point. (More than a few agencies have been known to just make shit up.) Where it gets dicey is extrapolating all that data about Sloane and assuming it's true for an entire group of women that the data says is just like her. As Viktor Mayer-Schönberger and Kenneth Cukier, the authors of *Big Data*, are fond of saying, big data knows the what, but it doesn't know the why. These women may share similar traits with Sloane (the what), but nobody knows why, or even whether the assumption is correct that they're just like her in reality. After the persona is presented to the client, it is usually accepted as fact. The client then prepares a strategy to target Sloane and all women like her, resulting in millions of dollars spent on the creation and distribution of relevant advertising and content targeted at those women. Now, if we were just talking marketing, this would be fine. Seriously. I don't want you to think I'm completely anti-data or anti-Facebook, because I'm not. I think Facebook and the other tech companies are doing a shitty thing that I'd like them to stop, but that doesn't mean I hate them or think their product is without any use. Twitter has provided a platform for voices previously unheard by the media to be heard, such as Black Lives Matter and LGBTQ comic book fans. Facebook can be very good at fostering a sense of community around particular topics and issues. And the data can be useful for some things. In marketing, you need to know who your audience is in order to create demand among them, but we're making some major assumptions here concerning the quality of the data being used. With marketing, again, that's fine because marketing allows for a lot of flexibility due to being mostly fancy bullshit. In a lot of respects, you can create Sloane through marketing and get your target customers to cluster around an identity they can relate to and even want to be, through your email or search engine optimization (SEO) efforts. If you are well organized, as my friend Jeremy Simon pointed out, and if your company is organized the right way, then getting as much intelligence as you can on something like a customer's purchase data (which Amazon has) is excellent and highly useful. The problems begin with companies that are not well set up, or others that are just randomly gathering raw data because they saw another company in their space gathering data too.

That's the difference, I think, between marketing and advertising. In marketing, you can create a Sloane, but in advertising, you pay to reach people who you think are like her. So, advertising is a different story, and that's what we want to focus on here. Because while the data being collected may be interesting and potentially useful for marketers, that's not always the case once we switch gears and talk about the part of the advertising industry that intersects with these tech companies. And advertising is always the bigger story of the two because it makes up 19 percent of America's GDP, according to Adweek. That's what's fuelling a lot of value around your data. Because we're now talking $3.4 trillion getting flushed down the drain to advertise to a customer persona that may or may not exist, and that has major ripple effects on other industries, including the media and tech. Advertisers may pull their funding from *Newsweek*, for example, and through using programmatic advertising, advertise to people like Sloane on any website the data suggests that she frequently visits. *Newsweek* then has to cut staff, or maybe even shut down from the loss of advertising revenue, and websites get that money instead. 'Free' isn't actually free. You also get what you pay for, which is something my Mom is fond of saying immediately after something falls apart in front of her.

If I'm Amazon, and I tell you that you can better target women like Sloane by paying for advertisements on my platform, you're going to pull that money from other places like print advertising. I don't want to go off on too much of a tangent here, because I did it in my last book, but if you want to know why newspapers are struggling, it's not because people aren't reading them. It's because there's less and less advertising revenue available to them, despite the fact that print has a higher rate of recall and people are more engaged with it when they're reading it. Therefore, the corporate consolidation that has gone on in the media world has led to a lot of spreadsheet jockeys making decisions for their companies. And since those people see marketing as an expense and not an investment, they're going to put their money into something that is cheap and easily quantifiable—even if the numbers are complete nonsense and the people they're targeting don't exist.

On the wrong path

In the tech industry, another thing that fuels the value of your data is the amount of money flowing into a lot of these companies in the form of venture funding and dreams of going public. I tell you all this to stress that a lot of money changes hands in exchange for your data, and that in turn entices even more efforts, creepy or otherwise, to collect it in order to keep the flow of advertising money coming. We'll close this chapter with one more example.

To understand how your data is used to grow tech companies, let's take a look at Path and their use of Rapleaf, a data broker that eventually got itself banned from Facebook by being a little too aggressive with its data collection methods (and the fact that *The Wall Street Journal* wrote about them). Path was an app that received a lot of hype when it was first announced, but then it fell off the face of the Earth. Path was meant to be a private social network that could connect users with only their friends and family. Despite the hype, the product never caught on in the States. However, in Silicon Valley, when you have a lot of venture capital funding—as Path did with $66 million raised—failure is not a viable option. So, in their desperate quest for survival, Path engaged in some 'creepy' behaviour, like spamming people via text message at six in the morning. This is about as unwelcome a thing to wake up to as receiving an unsolicited picture of some stranger in a gimp mask on OkCupid.

But before we can talk about what Path did, we need to talk about Rapleaf, since most people have no idea they existed back then. Founded in 2005, Rapleaf partnered with various websites and apps to collect user information through a variety of methods—up to and including straight-up paying for it. In other, more sneaky cases, every time a user entered information into a website or app partnered with Rapleaf, including, of course, Facebook, those companies shared that piece of information with Rapleaf. Rapleaf then used it to connect the dots around the web and see what else it could find out about that user. The compiled information was then sold to third parties. When TowerData, an 'email intelligence' company, purchased Rapleaf, the company claimed Rapleaf had a database containing 80 percent of the email addresses used in the United States. This database was used by tech companies to grow their businesses, including Path.

Path, in their desperation to make new money and justify the money they'd already raised, allegedly used Rapleaf to broaden their outreach efforts by targeting users who might respond favourably to unsolicited messages sent to them by the service. This idea didn't come from nowhere. One trick Facebook used to grow its platform was to acquire email service providers and other tech companies overseas, outside of the media's view, that would provide them with the means to acquire numerous email addresses that they could then target to promote Facebook. One such company, the Malaysia-based Octazen, was a notorious scraper of other people's data (including emails), and Facebook acquired it in 2010. If you don't remember hearing about the Octazen purchase in all the stories marvelling at Facebook's rapid rise in popularity, that's because the story got little play and was quietly swept under the rug in the hype and hysteria surrounding Facebook's alleged viral growth. I guess that part of *The Social Network* movie got cut, you know? (Perhaps no small coincidence, but Dave Morin who co-founded Path used to work at Facebook.)

Although Path was unsuccessful, the point to take away here is that in order to grow its business, Path resorted to using creepy methods to collect personal data, and then spammed those people with unwanted messages, like Facebook and many other companies in the Valley did in the name of 'growth hacking'. All of this has been common practice for over twenty years among American tech companies dating back to Hotmail. They did this to justify their perceived future valuation, the millions invested in them, and the lofty expectations that came along with that. Path, unfortunately, was not doing anything unusual. They were just the one that got caught. Kind of like Bernie; not Sanders, Madoff.

CHAPTER SUMMARY

➤ Your data is valuable. It powers the multibillion-dollar advertising industry and tech industry. We're talking about trillions of dollars and thousands of jobs here.

➤ Because trillions of dollars are at stake, companies can, and often do, resort to 'creepy' means in order to obtain your information. More often than not, this is done without your explicit consent.

➤ The 'creepy' behaviour occurs because of a lack of sufficient legislation and governmental or independent oversight to protect consumers. The behaviour is not illegal, but it probably should be. And sometimes people straight-up lie about it to sweep it under the rug. There was a company featured on a popular ABC show involving businesses whose public story about how they got so big does not at all reflect what they really did to grow. This particular company told people they were solving a problem, and people were excited and talked about the service, but the reality is that they scraped (collected) emails from publicly available college databases and then spammed the shit out of those students until the students signed up for their service. In that case, their actions did cross into legally questionable conduct, but good luck getting anyone to talk about it unless you know the people who did it.

CHAPTER SIX

YOUR DATA, BUT NOT YOUR CHOICE

Where your privacy is concerned, it's not just the data you submit—or what gets scooped up by a hidden service like Octazen—that should worry you. Personal privacy is a serious matter. However, as we move toward more and more items in and around our homes and on our bodies having their own Internet connection, it's important to keep in mind that each of those nearly nine billion devices are collecting and transmitting data about you too. And this data presents another opportunity for the violation of your privacy and the potential use of your data against you. In theory, there shouldn't be a problem with owning and using something like an Apple Watch or an Amazon Echo, but like they once said on *The Simpsons*, "in theory, Communism works."

The idea of an 'Internet of Things' might seem completely foreign. And that's OK. Much like 'The Cloud' and 'Big Data', the Internet of Things is really just a fancy name to describe Internet-connected tools that find their way into your home, your body, and your city. The term can also be used to describe those awesome refrigerators that tell you when your milk has expired and even log into your Amazon account to order more milk for you. Even if self-stocking Frigidaires aren't your style, some of you might be driving around in cars right now that are Internet-enabled. Or have devices installed in your cars by your insurance companies, with your consent, to report your travel data back to them in exchange for a discount on your premium. In keeping with using *Simpsons* quotes in this chapter: "Ooh, they have the Internet on computers now". At the time, in 1997, that joke was hilarious because you could only access the Internet from a desktop computer. But today, and going forward into the future, it's reasonable to believe that more than a few people would be surprised to learn that the Internet on all their devices could also be accessed with a computer. Scary, I know, but we're getting there. I was just told recently that movies from the 1980s qualify as 'classic movies'. So, I'm not kidding when I tell you that, some day not very far away, kids are going to be surprised to learn that the Internet is also available on their computer...assuming they even own a computer at all. That means you have to take pretty seriously the prospect of everything in your house, on your body, and in your neighbourhood, being connected to the Internet. That's no longer a discussion for the future—it's a discussion for now. (And remember, there are sensors and cameras everywhere now too. That's not hysteria or science fiction; it's fact.)

You might imagine that a lot of issues surface when talking about data collection and privacy where this new frontier is concerned. For the sake of clarity, I will refer to the data collected by most of your personal devices as 'dynamic' data because that data changes over time. We're not talking static data here (i.e. data that won't change, like your Social Security Number). Dynamic data refers to information that closely reflects your everyday reality. In other words, the food you order through Seamless, the series you watch on Netflix, your house temperature, your heart rate and pulse. These things are dynamic. One example: every morning for the past month, I have had to take my blood pressure, pop some medication, and take my blood pressure again. My blood pressure changes, hopefully, and I have to log this data to give to my cardiologist. My blood pressure is a great example of dynamic data, and since I log my blood pressure into a Google Sheet, Google now has a running record of the changes in my blood pressure. That data is dynamic: it's different a half-hour later than what it was before.

These are some questions that should come to your mind when thinking about the dynamic data you produce:

- What if that data is intercepted by a third party?
- Who pays to store all that dynamic data?
- What company wants to store this data?
- What decisions are going to be made with that data?
- Who owns it?
- What do they plan to do with it?
- Is my data encrypted?
- Is my data hosted on a regularly updated server?

Are you in good hands?

A great example of a company interested in dynamic data is Nest, the Alphabet-owned division that explained it "takes privacy seriously"…despite having experienced a security breach involving your data, sharing other data with Google when they were still independent from them, and having numerous rumoured data-sharing partnerships with other companies interested in your data as well. Not to mention the Nest Cam, the always-on camera that you can access remotely—which, by the way, is also storing that video footage for you to access later in The Cloud. Where is that footage being stored and who else has access to it? Even if you're not overly concerned about the Nest thermostat, you might want to be concerned about that camera. Especially now that Nest has rolled out a version of the camera that's made to be placed outside your home in the name of security. I'm not saying there's anything wrong with these products; I'm just saying you should be mindful of who has access to the information those products are taking in—especially if that information is going to be used against you, which is one of the few other credible reasons that you should care about all this privacy stuff to begin with. You may enjoy the free stuff now, but the use of your data by all these other parties is certain to bite you in the ass later, and not in a sexy way.

As just one example, we know that companies have attempted to correlate your FICO score with the kind of friends you have on Facebook. But there are many more ways that data you don't think about can be used against you. Let's look at your heart rate and pulse as a form of dynamic data that's being collected and reported. If you have John Hancock as your health insurance provider, they will give you a discount if you let them monitor your Fitbit data. And on the face of it, that doesn't sound too bad. Health insurance is expensive, so who doesn't want to save a little money? Now, let's say you develop a condition, like I have, where you need to track your blood pressure every morning, take medication, and monitor the resulting changes. During that time, John Hancock decides to adjust your rates, but this time, they're increasing them because they now know you have Autonomic Neuropathy. How would they know? Through the data shared with them by Google Sheets, your search results and browsing habits, Fitbit, or the Apple Watch concerning your health. Suddenly that 15 percent discount evaporates and you're paying twice what you were paying before, if they even want to continue insuring you at all.

I'm not saying John Hancock or other insurance companies will do this to you, but the door is certainly open for insurance providers to do so now that dynamic data collection from devices like Fitbit and Nest is becoming more common. The door is also open—and some suspect insurance companies have already walked through it—for data to be passed around by companies like Experian and Facebook that could be used to charge you higher premiums (or interest rates) based on the information they learn about you, if they want to do business with you in the first place.

If you were to look at this scenario from an insurance company's perspective, using your data against you may be terrible customer service, but adjusting the premiums of customers they know are getting sick could mean less money spent to care for a customer as their health gets worse. When I went in for what turned out to be two back-to-back heart surgeries (one scheduled, the other a fun surprise), the insurance company paid out $300,000 to the hospital and its doctors. Now imagine if the insurance company had decided to drop my coverage prior to the surgery because my data had detected a change in my heart rate that set off a red flag in their system. Guess who would have been on the hook for that $300,000 bill? The savings to more than a few Ivy League MBAs, spreadsheet jockeys, and shareholders outweigh offering terrible customer service like this to you and me. More often than not, when a big company offers crappy customer service, you can bet it's because some spreadsheet jockey said "it doesn't scale" and couldn't justify the cost, failing to see customer service as an investment rather than an expense. To make matters worse, algorithms can—and often are—utilized to sort customers based on the data that companies have gathered on them. Meaning that in some instances, a wealthy client or customer may get priority treatment while another, less well-off client, may be doomed to an infinite hell of one automated voice menu after another. All of this is based on the data collected on those customers without their knowledge. Taken to an extreme (and people far smarter than myself have started making this argument), your data can, has been, and will be used to discriminate against you in ways that no person should ever have to be.

I mention this because tech companies appeal to spreadsheet jockeys, since they have numbers and data points they can readily quantify. That's what makes everything I'm telling you in this book work. If we can immediately measure it, we'll make decisions based on it, and that can and does often lead to bad things happening. We replace the humanity and long-term thinking with making decisions almost entirely based on what data we've collected, even if that data only presents a partial or imperfect picture. And as most people in the big data field will tell you, imperfect or close enough is what you're going to get more and more of in terms of the results this data produces. That's sort of terrifying when you're talking about people's lives here. As Cathy O'Neil points out in *Weapons of Math Destruction*, there are far greater issues to be concerned with as well. For example, if the police have access to your data and an algorithm says you're likely to murder someone, they may pay you a visit to tell you they're watching you. That might sound like something out of the awful Tom Cruise film *Minority Report*, but this is something that's already here. And what's alarming is that it's not people looking at this data and weighing it against other factors, it's people just looking at the data and going, "Sure. I completely trust what this algorithm is telling me." We worship this stuff, and when it comes to data, we really shouldn't. Data can be a useful tool in solving problems, but it's not the solution.

There are also questions about the interception of dynamic data. What happens when someone who isn't supposed to get that data does get it? The idea of someone hacking into a pacemaker and using it to kill their target figured prominently in a storyline for the Showtime series *Homeland*, but it's not as fictional as it sounds. Former

Vice President Dick Cheney openly worried about his pacemaker being hacked. And I'm not going to lie to you, I've had plenty of heart issues in my life, so the idea of someone hacking into a pacemaker is definitely a factor in me not getting one just yet. Remember this: if it's connected to the Internet, it can probably be hacked. As we head into 2018, there's not a day that passes without a news story about someone or something being hacked. Imagine now that file with all your data floating around, and some asshole decides to steal your identity. It sounds ridiculous when I write it, but more than 145.5 million Americans are facing precisely that thanks to the Equifax data breach and the comical ineptitude that ensued after the revelation. This is no longer a joke or a paranoid fantasy that your silver-hoarding uncle likes to tell.

If you're using an Apple Watch, or any other device to monitor your health, what happens if that data is scooped up on your work's WiFi connection and your boss decides to fire you because of it? Think about that for a moment. Why do you think stores offer you free WiFi in the first place? It's so they can track you around the store and scoop up all the data you're transmitting while using it. They're not offering you free WiFi out of the kindness of their hearts. Corporations don't have hearts. Neither does your boss!

But let's talk about your employer and their WiFi for a moment. Let's say they know you're going to miss a lot of time because of an emerging health issue detected by the data they've scooped up. Or, what if your employer was able to tell you were pregnant before you knew it yourself and then decided to force you out of your job? It sounds like something out of a dystopian novel but, unfortunately, with all this new dynamic data collection going on, it's entirely possible and increasingly likely. Remember, we're less than a century removed from assembly-line workers having their managers follow them around with stopwatches to time and measure their performance. What I'm saying is not unreasonable to consider. Especially when one company, Tesco, was accused of asking their employees to wear armbands to track how hard they were working during their shifts. This created a situation where Tesco employees were allegedly punished for taking unplanned bathroom breaks. The year this happened? 2013.

With luck, none of this will ever happen in your neck of the woods. Or, if it does, you'll be offered some kind of method to contest what's being said. If some algorithm says you shouldn't be hired for a job or be offered an apartment, and no human was involved in that decision-making process, you should have the right to contest the algorithm's finding. This seems like a no-brainer, but not enough people fully appreciate what's being done with all the data they're just giving away. Especially when that data comes back to haunt them later.

Hopefully, the right regulations will be set in place, strengthening the areas where current US law doesn't cover this sort of thing. The European Union continues to be the leader on protecting the privacy of their citizens, so models do exist for governments and lawyers around the world to guide them through the process of protecting our dynamic data, as well as our static data. But it's important to understand that when we're talking about privacy, we're not just talking about the assumed-private info you enter into platforms like Facebook. We're talking about larger issues that could potentially have ramifications far beyond your use of the Internet on your phone. We're talking about the devices in your home, on your body, and all around you too.

CHAPTER SUMMARY

➢ There's static data, and there's dynamic data. Collecting both is bad, but the collection of dynamic data is going to become especially troublesome for us in the twenty-first century. We have to figure out who keeps hold of this data (such as details about your blood pressure), what they're doing with it, where they're storing it and, most important of all, who they're sharing it with. This data could be used to harm you in a variety of ways, and there's little on the books at the moment to protect you.

➢ I mentioned earlier that if you use the Internet, you have no privacy. I want to add that if you use the Internet, you should have no expectation of your data being safe, because it probably won't be encrypted, and it's too tempting for criminals not to target.

➢ The kind of dynamic data that can be picked up about you is kind of crazy when you think about it. There are now algorithms out there that can allow a Wi-Fi network to detect whether you're still breathing. That may be great in the nursing home you stuck grandma in, but not so much when that technology is being used to track your movements all over the office, or how often you use the bathroom.

CHAPTER SEVEN

A PLACE FOR YOUR STUFF

The comedian George Carlin, in the prime of his career, had a wonderful routine called *A Place for My Stuff*. The 'place' starts out very small, but slowly gets bigger and bigger as Carlin details the need for everything he owns to have its own place where he can get to it. And what does Carlin explain is the inevitable consequence of continued accumulation? The need for an even bigger place to hold more stuff.

Carlin died in 2008, so it's not known what he would have said about The Cloud but, digitally speaking, The Cloud gives us all a place for our stuff. As you might have guessed by this point in the book, there are some issues with trusting the companies like Dropbox, Apple, and Amazon who provide cloud storage for your 'stuff'. The Cloud describes the space allotted to users where they can upload and store their files remotely. In other words, to store those files on a computer that is not their own. That's all it is. The Cloud is just a clever marketing term to describe storing your 'stuff' on someone else's 'thing', or server, to put it in terms George Carlin would have appreciated.

Now, to be fair to the providers of Cloud-based storage who may come and go as you read this, The Cloud is a perfectly legitimate and mostly safe place for your stuff. There is nothing to fear from relying on The Cloud. In fact, this is a point I've made throughout this book: I'm not saying any of these products are inherently bad or creepy. The companies can, and often do, act in a creepy way, but if you want to use Facebook or Apple's iCloud, go for it. Just be educated about what's going on with your data and how it's being used.

But, in keeping with the theme of this book, there are some issues that should still be addressed. Specifically, although these Cloud storage companies provide a great service, you shouldn't trust them to have your best interests at heart when it comes to your 'stuff'. In fact, you shouldn't assume you have any privacy at all concerning what you've uploaded to someone else's servers. Remember: if it involves the Internet, assume nothing you do on it is private.

Who do you trust with your stuff?

Back in 2014, the world learned that a ring of hackers was breaking into the iCloud accounts of female celebrities, downloading their private (and often nude) photos, and sharing the photos amongst themselves. One of the members of the ring decided to post the photos they had on 4chan, a web-based image board. Once the photos hit 4chan, they made their way to Reddit, and from there, to the rest of the world. This is because Reddit is often a source of news for bloggers and journalists. But how did the hackers get those photos in the first place?

When we talk about privacy, we have to talk about trust. Who do you trust with your 'stuff'? In this case, we see that these celebrities placed their trust in Apple. They thought their stuff was secure when stored within Apple's iCloud server. Except it totally wasn't. And Apple is a company that tells people, right on their page about privacy (at www.apple.com/privacy/) that they, as a company, believe privacy to be a fundamental human right. (LOL.)

In fact, not long after the leaked nude photos began to circulate, we learned that Apple knew of the exploit the hackers used to access the accounts of the celebrities and did nothing to fix it. Think about that for a second. Millions of people store their stuff using Apple's iCloud service. According to comScore, there were over 85 million iPhones in the United States as of December 2016. Apple knew there was a flaw that would allow for hackers to break in and access people's stuff. And their response was not only to do nothing, but as the nude photos circulated, Apple claimed their service was secure while they finally got around to fixing the exploit they had known about months before. (Apple shouldn't be the only one with some blame here, however; Reddit kept the nude celebrity photos up for a week before shutting down the subreddits housing the photos, thereby benefitting from the sheer amount of traffic generated during this time.)

Later that same year, Dropbox had a security breach of its own. What happened was, either hackers stole usernames and passwords from Dropbox, or they stole usernames and passwords from other services and, using those usernames and passwords, were able to access Dropbox accounts. This allowed the hackers to pull anything and everything they'd like from Dropbox accounts as long as the accounts were compromised. Was Dropbox lying when they told everyone they weren't hacked, the way Apple did? Or were the hackers lying, as Dropbox claimed? It's not clear, but either way, it doesn't matter. Throughout this book, you'll find numerous instances of hacks and security breaches occurring because nobody wanted to pay to update the security software. That sounds messed up, don't you think? When we're talking about a multibillion-dollar company, or at least one that's valued as such, you'd think little things like this would be taken care of, but they're not. Not often, anyway. And we're all just sort of blindly trusting these companies to protect our stuff for us. Why? You really have to ask yourself why these tech companies all get a pass for stupid, predatory things, but the second some other non-tech company messes up (like Mattel), we're all over them crying "No! Bad company!"

Look, I love Dropbox. I love Apple, I really mean that, they make great stuff — but this is some amateur-hour-level shit right here, and there's no excuse for it. And if you want an extreme example of the other problem when it comes to companies getting hacked and being deceitful about it, Yahoo! grossly misinformed the public about the number of accounts that were compromised, finally admitting (of course, only after their multibillion-dollar purchase by Verizon went through) that every single Yahoo! account had been compromised. Marissa Mayer, who was heralded as the saviour of Yahoo! when she first took the reins of the company, received a $23 million golden parachute after the Verizon purchase was completed. The security breach of every single Yahoo! account, as well as the company downplaying how bad the breach was, happened on her watch.

That leads us to another rule you should remember: do not take what tech companies tell the public at face value. Ever. (The same is true for hackers too.) The simple truth—and this isn't an indictment of the people that work for these companies, just the culture that surrounds these companies in general—is that they lie about everything. How the company grew is one example, such as when Dropbox and their 'growth hacker' friends told everyone they took off because of how wonderful and viral their product was, but you really have to dig to discover that a large chunk of their installs came from overseas with Android manufacturers pre-installing Dropbox on phones. To say nothing of all the press the founders of Dropbox got after they turned down an acquisition offer from Steve Jobs in 2009. There is the myth, and then there's the reality. Companies also lie about how many people use their service. Do you really think Facebook has over a billion active users? Let's assume they're not factoring spammers and fake accounts, OK, but how do they qualify an active user? If your answer is "I don't know", you'd be correct, because only Facebook knows. Twitter, Instagram, and Snapchat, among many, many others have all been caught at one point or another lying about how many active users they have. As I write this, Snapchat's parent company is being sued for inflating their user numbers in the run-up to their IPO. (You also saw that above with Apple. Publicly, Apple said their service was secure, but they knew about the exact security exploit used to access the leaked photos.) And here you have Dropbox, a company that, at the time of this writing, has a multibillion-dollar valuation, saying their system is secure while hackers are saying otherwise. Regardless of the truth, the end result of the Dropbox hack was that a lot of people had to change their passwords and had their accounts compromised. The sad thing is that by the time you read this, you can swap out Apple and Dropbox and replace them with any other company that's suffered a massive data breach and then proceeded to downplay or outright lie about how bad the breach was, or question whether it happened at all. Why is it OK for us to all laugh at President Trump when he declares that articles about him are 'fake news', but the tech companies and other large corporations get a pass when doing the same? Because we like the things we buy from them? Really? That's what we're going with? Sure, Trump is an asshole, but did you ever stop to think that maybe some of the people at Apple are too?

But, say by some miracle you stumble upon a cloud services provider who reports and fixes all known security flaws promptly, and who seems to have (gasp!) your interests in line with their interests. Even that miraculous yet-to-be-seen company will still have to contend with criminals—and that means you'll have to contend with criminals, too. As I've laid out for you in this book, your data—your 'stuff'— has an incredibly high value ascribed to it. Think about all the Driver's License data and Social Security numbers that were stolen as part of the Equifax breach, as just one example. That's gold for fraudsters and other criminal types. Never put it past a rogue criminal enterprise, company, or data broker to want to break into a cloud-based service in order to access the data within it.

As I mention elsewhere, it's not just the criminals we should be concerned about. The tech companies, in my mind anyway, are public enemy number one. Especially since they have so much to gain from our data. In many cases, their very survival depends on it. And, following them are the disgruntled ex-employees who often appear behind some of the security breaches we hear about in the news. Here's another good rule to remember from this book along with "Nothing you do on the Internet is private" and "Your data is not secure no matter what anyone tells you": the majority of the time you read about some massive data breach or hack, it was because of the involvement of an ex-employee of the company—which again reaffirms my belief that people are dicks. But seriously, if you watch a lot of cop shows like *Chicago P.D.*, *Lucifer*, or any of the multitude of *Law and Order* episodes that air today, you'll notice that it's usually the third person introduced in that episode who is the guilty party. (Now that I've told you that, I may have ruined your ability to enjoy police procedurals forever. My bad.) So, it's sort of the same deal here; when you hear about these hacks or security breaches, it's usually the ex-employee who did it. This is sadly predictable, is what I'm saying.

Just to build on that point, as sophisticated as some of

the software and algorithms (or recipes!) that companies use to protect our data online are, human error or human malice is a frequent contributor to major data breaches. In the case of the 145 million-plus Americans who were impacted by the Equifax data breach in late 2017, it turns out the breach could have been prevented months earlier …if the people working there had bothered to update the security software. In the case of the hack involving the consulting firm Deloitte, had they enabled two-factor authentication, they could have protected the plans of some of their biggest clients from being stolen. And here's the kicker: one of the areas that Deloitte, a firm with $38 billion in revenue, consults in? If you guessed cyber security, congratulations. I owe you a high five.

One of the things George Carlin always talked about was how respect should be earned, not given. Trust works the same way. You should not trust the companies that you use to store your stuff in The Cloud to have your best interests at heart or to be looking out for you. Same deal when it comes to the app makers and creators of other platforms you choose to use on the Internet. If you're not watching your own back, you could find yourself in a lot of trouble.

CHAPTER SUMMARY

➢ Assume nothing is private. Nothing you store in The Cloud is private. That doesn't mean don't use The Cloud, it just means: know what you're getting yourself into, and think twice about what you upload to it.

➢ Tech companies lie. Apple knew about the exploit

that led to the access and spread of nude celebrity photos. (Not to mention plenty of other people's photos too.) They did nothing until the issue made the news. Dropbox, if you believe the hackers, claimed they were secure while clearly not being so. Most businesses don't have your best interests at heart. If it saves them money to not update their software and other security methods, you can bet they're not going to do it. If there's a quick fix we can make immediately it can be to heavily fine these lax companies hundreds of millions of dollars for data breaches.

➤ Common sense can protect you. When it comes to storing your stuff online, you should enable two-factor authentication and make sure you have a decent password that you change once a year. Hint: '123456' and 'Password' are not decent passwords, despite being some of the most common choices among Internet users. A good password is at least eight characters long and uses a nice mix of letters, numbers, and symbols, like this: 'H1ll0H0w@reY0u'? Unless you're writing that kind of password down, however, you're better off using a random configuration of words instead. The famous example from the tech-savvy, and hilarious, webcomic XKCD is a great case in point: 'Correct Horse Battery Staple'. That's memorable and hard for a hacker to guess because it's completely nonsensical.

➤ Lie. When filling out your answers to security questions, you should lie. Obviously, keep track somewhere (offline, preferably) of what those lies are, but the more truthful you are, the easier it is to hack you. Remember: just because a website or some other device or platform asks for your information, doesn't mean you have to give them actual information.

CHAPTER EIGHT

BIG DATA, BIGGER BUSINESS

Earlier I explained that your data is valuable, and that's why so many non-government entities want to invade your privacy. The more data that companies accumulate, the more money they make off you. This has been in practice since the beginning of the Internet boom, when Netscape Navigator was harvesting data on their users. In theory, by using an Internet platform or app's service, you're aware of what the company is doing to collect your data since you 'read' the Terms of Service. But in reality nobody reads these agreements, and every company knows that. Companies, especially those that collect data by being creepy, have a great incentive to change their Terms of Service often—and without warning—to justify some of their more dubious data-collection practices. In 2011, for example, Dropbox altered its Terms of Service, briefly, to claim they owned all your stuff that was uploaded to their service. In October 2017, Patreon changed its privacy policy to prohibit the use of their site to support adult content creators. The contract you agree to, the Terms of Service, may in theory protect you, but it actually does the opposite, since it can be changed on a whim.

So, here I want to provide you with some examples of this invasion of privacy, as well as outline what's going on within the world of the tech that fuels this behaviour.

Creepy behaviour

No matter how evolved we like to think we are, we still very much operate under the ancient credo of 'Monkey see, monkey do'. For example, if you see your friends passing around a funny video, you're likely to pass on that same video, partly because you think the video is indeed funny but, mostly, because you want others to think you're funny. Your friend then gets the video and goes through the same process, usually sharing it for the same reason. We're herd animals, even when we pretend to be individuals. For those of you who watch *South Park*, there's an episode where Stan goes and joins the goth kids at school. They all want to be non-conformists but, in doing so, the goth kids all look, act, and talk the same, a point Stan makes. In a lot of ways, we're all those goth kids, whether we like it or not. And that goes too for employees of large companies in a very competitive space. So, if a large multibillion-dollar tech company is doing something creepy to collect data, then it's more than reasonable to assume smaller companies looking to achieve multibillion-dollar valuations themselves will do the same. Path's Dave Morin provided us with one such example already, but let me give you two more examples from the rich history of the Internet.

AOL

These days it's easy to forget AOL exists, especially now that it goes by the super-dumb Orwellian name of Oath. But, if you rewind the clock to 1994, back when you needed AOL or a similar service provider to access the Internet, AOL was massive. At one point, AOL was so big, they bought Time Warner (not the other way around, as is often reported). How did AOL become so valuable? They made money from people by using advertising, branded partnerships, and subscription services. The company very quickly developed the nasty habit of collecting and selling their users' data without permission. In 1996, after the media called them out on this practice, it appeared that AOL backed off. Three years later, however, AOL actually revised their Terms of Service—without informing their users!—to allow the company to sell user data to their business partners without consequence. They backed off after another media backlash, which as I hope you're starting to see, is an incredibly common pattern. Even today, as we saw with the Samsung Smart TV incident—where it was revealed by Samsung in their privacy policy that the Smart TV's remote includes a microphone that potentially could listen in and record your conversations while you're holding the remote—a company will try to collect data in a creepy way, be confronted by media or consumers, and then back off, only to try again later. AOL is important to mention here, because it's one of the first instances of an Internet platform selling user data without the user's permission or knowledge. Today, that's common practice. Just ask Google and Amazon who, under new EU privacy laws, will have to inform customers that their Echo and Home devices are always listening to them, no matter what those companies say about the devices only activating when they hear their watch word. Speaking of Google...

Google

To provide just one example of the numerous instances where Google has done something creepy, I'd like to mention the often-reported Street View incident from 2010. First, because I just told you the Google Home devices are sort of creepy, but also because this is at the top of my list of all-time creepy things Google has done to gather your data.

In 2010, as Google vans were driving around the country taking those highly useful Street View pictures that can be found when using Google Maps, the company was also scooping up any data that anyone had received or sent using nearby unsecured Wi-Fi connections. In other words, if someone had just sent a non-password-protected nude pic to someone else over a Wi-Fi connection, it was very likely that Google now had that picture and could use it in some capacity. Google, for their part, tried to claim that they'd collected the data accidentally. As time went on, Google changed their story and said everything sent over unsecured Wi-Fi was public and, therefore, their data harvesting was not illegal in the first place. US Judge James Ware disagreed, and eventually Google apologized, paid a fine, and claimed to have stopped collecting data via Street View vans. However, that is not the end of this story. In 2017, Google is still appealing the case, and they even tried to have it heard before the Supreme Court. (The case in question is *Joffe v. Google, Inc.* for those curious to find it.) Where the case currently stands, the judge determined that Google's activity was, in fact, illegal. Consider for a moment that this practice was something Google had claimed to have been doing accidentally, then claimed they were no longer doing, but still tried to contest the issue in court later. That should strike anyone as a bit odd. If Google knew that what they were doing was wrong, and claimed to have stopped doing it, why continue to contest the legality of their data collection methods? Remember, again, just how valuable your data is. And, even though Google has already made many people wealthy, it still has a business to run and obligations to fulfil for its shareholders. Being one of the most prominent tech companies today, like AOL was back in 1994, it's reasonable to assume that other tech companies are observing Google's behaviour and have opted to take similar approaches to collecting your data. Monkey see, monkey do.

Foursquare

Another quick example of the monkey credo is Foursquare. They, like Twitter, burst onto the tech scene with a lot of tech and mainstream media attention before quickly floundering. In their defense, FourSquare changed their business model and are now doing quite well for themselves...by selling your data. Surprise! But that's not why I brought them up. In a similar fashion to Google's harvesting of data available on the routers of unsuspecting users, Foursquare made a change in their app to allow it to constantly track users. This was a quiet change from what the app originally allowed users to do, which was to 'check in' upon arriving at a location. And although that may not sound so bad, I haven't mentioned the best part: this tracking, in the words of the blog *Consumerist*, "doesn't just take place when mobile users open the app, though. It takes place literally any time their phones are powered on. Even if you've just booted up your phone and have forgotten that Foursquare was ever installed on there, it's now watching where you go." The connection between Foursquare and Google? Google had purchased what was the precursor to Foursquare, Dodgeball, and the Dodgeball co-founders left Google after some time to start FourSquare. Monkey see (Google). Monkey do (Foursquare). More recently, Uber's app tracked users' locations for up to five minutes, and perhaps longer, after they completed their ride. The odds are good that some of your apps are doing this to you right now. All to collect some of that sweet, sweet revenue associated with your data. Although I could write a book on Uber's shadiness alone (one such book already exists, written by the executive editor of *Fortune*, Adam Lashinsky), here are a few more examples from recent years of companies screwing around with your data.

Instagram. Think back to early 2013. Some of you might remember a controversy, similar to what we saw with AOL, involving a change in Instagram's Terms of Service. Before a media backlash occurred, Instagram had language in their Terms of Service that stated: "To help us deliver interesting paid or sponsored content or promotions, you agree that a business or other entity may pay us to display your username, likeness, photos (along with any associated metadata), and/or actions you take, in connection with paid or sponsored content or promotions, without any compensation to you." Why? Because, of course, your username, likeness, and photos are all the more valuable to businesses when they can associate them with their brands. This, by the way, is something Instagram's owner, Facebook, does today with ads on their site. All thanks to the Terms of Service. So, if you're wondering why your name is sometimes used to endorse a product you may or may not have heard of in your friend's newsfeed, now you know why.

PayPal. In 2015, PayPal modified their Terms of Service to allow them to add users' email addresses and phone numbers to a list that would essentially be spammed by the company. That seems relatively innocuous, until you remember that the US government has cracked down on telemarketing recently. This change to PayPal's Terms of Service worked essentially as an end run around the national Do Not Call list: i.e. not illegal, but certainly 'creepy' in giving them 'permission' to make unsolicited calls to their customers. Keep in mind that this manoeuvre on PayPal's part came just as they were splitting off from eBay and becoming their own company, meaning the economic incentive was there, and could be argued as being a contributing factor to this change in the Terms of Service (as it is with other companies mentioned in this book).

Spotify. Also in 2015, Spotify planned to change their Terms of Service and Privacy Policy so that Spotify could access (and I'm not kidding here) everything on your phone as well as track your location. After the usual backlash and reversal, Spotify backed off and 'clarified' that the location tracking was just for the 'Running' feature of the app—which seems like a legit defense, until you realize that Spotify still would have been tracking you even if you didn't use that feature. What exactly Spotify wanted with all the data is a bit more nebulous, but having read this chapter, you should be able to put two and two together. Hint: it's because they serve up targeted advertising to their free users, and the more data they have on those users, the more valuable that advertising capability is to advertisers. Of the 140 million people who use Spotify, myself included, only 50 million of them are premium subscribers. For the $30 billion company, that means the only real path to turning a profit (if they ever do so) is through advertising. That's a hell of an incentive to scoop up as much of your data as they can.

Why (else) do these companies do this?

Before we move on to other things, I wanted to say something about the world in which tech companies operate. Some may argue that people who work in Silicon Valley (or in tech generally) have a different understanding of privacy than the rest of the world. However, I never quite got where that argument came from, or what facts supported its existence. It's like when people claim the tech giants like Apple, Google, Facebook, Microsoft, and Amazon have been great for the American economy and proceed to offer no proof. They're job-killing tax avoiders who have ruthlessly cultivated a cute, friendly brand in an effort to make as much money as they can before we wake up and realize what they're doing. Also: a lot of them are hypocrites. Just ask Mark Zuckerberg and the house-buying spree he went on in his neighbourhood to protect his own privacy. This 'they have a different sense of privacy' nonsense seems more like something journalists and tech executives say about other tech executives in order to explain (or blame) behaviour that they personally don't endorse. What is true is that the tech world is filled with young people who have a bunch of money being dangled in front of them. When you're barely over twenty-one and looking at potentially making billions of dollars, the lines between right and wrong quickly become blurred. As I write this, entrepreneurs of all stripes are cramming words like 'machine learning' and 'artificial intelligence' into their PowerPoint presentations, despite having a company that does or uses neither. Remember: AI is used to describe things that don't exist. Machine learning is a real thing, but nowhere near as fancy as we want to think it is. Just look at how problematic Siri can be when you need to ask it a simple question and it miserably fails to answer it. (No, Siri, I said Tuesday, not tacos!)

All that exists in the tech world is the economic incentive to be creepy. If an app gains users quickly (and one tactic to do so involves getting access to your address book and spamming all your friends and family to join the app while keeping that data to sell later), then the company becomes more valuable to investors. So, there is almost always some incentive to violate privacy in the name of user growth. There is almost always some incentive to change the Terms of Service that nobody takes the time to read. If a high-flying start-up is dependent on advertising for revenue, then the incentive is to get all the data they can to make themselves more profitable to advertisers. Likewise, if a high-flying start-up is dependent on investors, then there's an incentive to collect user data to show to said investors that the start-up is viable because of the size of its database. Many start-ups begin their existence depending on either advertisers or investors for the bulk of their money—which means there is often an incentive to collect user data very early in their life. So, the hoovering of your personal data sometimes even begins on day one.

Every tech company with a business model built on advertising needs to be the company with the most useful data. The company with the most useful data wins. (Regardless of whether that data is actually worth a damn.) When winning involves a lack of ethics, and a lot of money is at stake, companies can be expected to do whatever it takes to win—your privacy be damned.

CHAPTER SUMMARY

➤ Don't feel bad for not reading the Terms of Service. Nobody does. And the TOS is often written in such a way to make it as impenetrable to readers as posisble. Companies assume you're not going to read it, which means they can get away with all sorts of shady stuff without you knowing, scooping up your data as they go.

➤ Here's some good news: over the past twenty years that tech companies have been doing creepy things, we observe a cycle where people get annoyed, and then companies back off from doing their creepy stuff. Or they get sued, which is what happened with Netscape. Now, I've said in this book that the companies will typically go back to being creepy the second that we stop looking. I stand by that; however, for the optimistic among us, there is a decent argument to be made that if we make enough noise as users of their sites, the companies will back off from such policies permanently.

CHAPTER NINE

THEY'RE ALL IN ON IT

It's easy to think that shopping online is something everyone does and is the wave of the future. In 2015, according to Pew, ten percent of all retail purchases were made online. I have no doubt that the number will tick up over time, although that ten percent represents billions of dollars ($350 billion, to be exact, in 2015) already…but it's that remaining 90 percent that seems to get no love these days in the press. Which is especially strange, when you consider that most people surveyed prefer to buy things offline, and when they do buy things online, they do so infrequently, or to get things no one cares about, like batteries.

The media would have you believe that Amazon is straight-up murdering brick-and-mortar stores. What's more likely is that the middle class of America is dying, and so are the stores that were there to support them. If brick-and-mortar was being killed for good, simply because of Amazon's sway, Amazon wouldn't have bought Whole Foods, and it wouldn't be opening brick-and-mortar stores of its own.

If we look just at comic book stores, for example, I don't have to go to them anymore because I use the Comixology app to buy my comics—so you would think that's why comic book stores are struggling. The reality is much more complex. The stores are struggling because of a monopoly that exists in the comics industry in terms of distribution (i.e. Diamond Comic Distributors), and because the store owners have to place huge orders on books that won't be out for months, regardless of whether those books are any good. That means the stores can, and often do, get stuck with crappy products that nobody wants, which they had to order anyway because that's how the comics industry works. Comic book fans still like going to the stores, and most who go there now pick up their weekly comics in addition to other things like graphic novels, toys, and other merchandise. Myth: Amazon is killing comic book stores. Reality: the comic book industry has a messed-up distribution pipeline that results in all sorts of messes and lost revenue, all of which puts many stores at the risk of closing down. Amazon is a factor, but not the sole cause.

By the way, I don't have a problem with the media, but after working as an editor and journalist for places like CBS College Sports and WonderHowTo.com, I've seen the guts of how our world works and, sometimes, we can be lazy. If it's easier, and faster, to put out a story saying Amazon is murdering retail, or that comic book stores are dying because everyone wants to shop online for everything, we'll do it. In almost every case, we're underpaid, overworked, have zero job security, and work for people obsessed only with metrics and not the truth. Let me put all this another way. While totally stipulating that Amazon is making billions (by the way, you can buy my comic *Vengeance, Nevada* exclusively through their Comixology app, so even I'm part of their machine), why do you think Borders went out of business? Was it because of Amazon or because of gross mismanagement and over-expansion, the same kind of overexpansion that's harming a lot of stores in the retail sector today? Hint: it wasn't Amazon. I can, and probably will, write a book about this, but my point here is that the tech companies want you to believe that online shopping is the wave of the future, even though most people—if given the choice—still prefer to purchase things at brick-and-mortar stores. The big deal breaker for most people is price. If they can get it for less online, they'll get it online. But, again, there's money in magic, and if we all say and think that Amazon is magic, then we're less likely to peek under the hood and see what they're really up to.

I'm not in the divination business, but I am willing to go out on a limb and say that the lifestyle of people buying things exclusively online won't ever be the dominant mode of retail and commerce. For one, it's been over twenty years since the media and tech companies started saying that, and it hasn't happened yet. For another, people are social creatures. We like to go outside. We like to do things. We like interacting with other people. This is how we're 'wired'. Given that fact, it's hardly surprising that most consumers prefer to shop in a brick-and-mortar store over doing the same online. Most people prefer the experience of going out, looking at the products, touching them, and comparing them to the other items around them. And, frankly, and also according to Pew, most of us just don't trust online reviews. We trust our friends and family.

There are many reasons for our brick-and-mortar preferences, including the above-mentioned social and tactile elements, but since this is a book on privacy, let me give you another reason that's relevant for our purposes: a lot of people are concerned about their data being properly protected, and they don't trust the online retailers (or the devices they use to visit those retailers) to provide that protection. So, in their mind, not only do you get a better shopping experience offline, but you're less likely to get creeped on as well. I wish that were true...

But here's the funny thing: the brick-and-mortar stores, in some cases at least, are getting just as invasive as their online counterparts as far as collecting data about you and violating your privacy goes. And a reason they're doing that, is so they can compete with Amazon.

It sure makes you wish for the good old days, right? My grandfather had a store in Brooklyn back in the 1930s, 1940s, and 1950s. Back then, you came into his store if you were looking for men's clothing (it was called the Empire Men's Shop), you bought what you wanted, and then you went home. Maybe, if my grandfather had to order something, he'd take your number and call you when the item came in. That was the entire relationship between him and the customer. And you know what the funny thing is? There were plenty of other places, probably less expensive, for customers to visit, but they went to see my grandfather because they formed a relationship with him. They were loyal customers. The kind that can keep a company in business for half a century. That's something that shouldn't be lost in this larger discussion of why companies want to gather so much data about you. A lot of it is done in the name of customer loyalty, and brand-building. The brands think all this data will help them form the same kind of relationship, digitally and offline, that my grandfather had with his customers. But they're woefully wrong in most cases, as I argued about earlier. Nothing beats human, live interaction—that's the glue that holds everything together. All the data in the world can't replace that. Remember: data is wonderful, but it's not the solution to your problems—it's only part of the solution. If you work in marketing and advertising, data is great at the top of the sales funnel, but it should not be your first and only point of reference with your customers.

I'm willing to bet that's still the case in a lot of small businesses across the world: good customer relations translate to lifelong customers. To these businesses, data is mostly meaningless beyond what's selling, what customers want, and what customers need. But, if you're a bigger company, even though your customers may not be pleased about being tracked, you'll have the tech companies breathing down your neck, pushing their technology onto you, as will your corporate managers and shareholders. I've sat in on more than one meeting involving a multibillion-dollar property that actively boasted about their use of iBeacon technology to track customers all over the store, thereby acquiring better and more accurate data than what could be scooped up on those customers through just tracking them using Wi-Fi. Why? Who cares? Serve your customers by talking to them, the way humans are supposed to! We don't want, or need, you to be Amazon. We already have one of those. But let's keep focused.

In-store tracking

In-store cameras and other devices like iBeacons aside, your smartphone is one of the best tracking devices ever made. Did you ever watch a TV show where one of the characters (who has a smartphone) gets planted with a tracking device? It's a common TV trope, but here's another funny thing: the tracking device is unnecessary. That's because if your phone is set to connect to Wi-Fi, it's constantly broadcasting itself to Wi-Fi networks around you, looking to connect to them. And since your phone has its own unique number, every time you go into the store, that same number appears, meaning it's easy to build up a pattern of shopping behaviour showing what you do while you're in the store. And to be clear here: we're talking about you. Yes, you. The person reading this. Your name is Jackie Bintz and your favourite book is *The Sirens of Titan* by Kurt Vonnegut. OK. Maybe not, but that unique number from your phone? Don't let anyone tell you the data is anonymized and we don't know where you live after visiting the store. We totally do. There are more than a few apps in the retail world that are constantly tracking your location, even when you're not in their store. So, somewhere between having your specific mobile phone number and the app activated and broadcasting your data, a store can pretty much tell when you're using the bathroom if they really wanted to. I wasn't kidding about the 'being followed into the bathroom' thing, you know. And yes, I wish I was kidding, but having worked on an app like this, I can tell you that I'm not.

Put another way: did you ever wonder how Google Maps knows how heavy the traffic is on your intended route? Yeah, they're not using satellites to figure that out, they're using your phone and everyone's phone around you that has that app installed.

For now, collecting your shopping patterns isn't terribly useful to the retailer in terms of targeting you specifically. They can make heat maps of the store and rearrange their inventory to spots that you and other customers frequent, but that's about it. However, as technology improves, you can bet on the store taking the next step. As just one example, the store could send you a push notification alerting you to a sale on the exact item you'd currently be looking at.

Now, is this a bad thing? Getting a coupon for the item you're looking at while you're in the store? I don't think it is. As it relates to dealings with tech companies, if we give them a piece of our data and privacy, they will give us a free service that's pretty good at what it does. We seem OK with that, but we're creeped out when tech companies are aggressive, unclear, or deceitful about what they're collecting, how, and who they're sharing it with. And that's where the problem rests. Since when was it a good idea for brick-and-mortar stores to be doing the same thing as Amazon? Not every dev team is going to deactivate a feature for being 'too creepy' in their location-tracking retail app. So, although a lot of privacy advocates will tell you 'a discussion needs happen', I don't agree. I think a store should tell you, in clear terms on their website and in their app, what they're doing and how to opt out if you don't like it. One thing I want to stress: the responsibility, and consequences, of collecting your data is on the company, not you. If anything, if a brick-and-mortar store wants your data so badly, they should pay you for it just like everyone else should.

Now, if that was me? I'll take a JCPenney coupon for that Iron Fist T-shirt any day of the week if I'm looking at it and have intent to buy it! (Hey, he's cool in the comics, OK?) But that's just me. I don't speak for everyone, nor do I want to. The option should be there for me to turn this feature on or off. And if the stores and tech companies don't want to give us this option, then the government or an independent organization will have to force them. This shouldn't be a discussion anymore. The rule should be Don't Be Creepy, and if you want to be creepy, you're either going to have to pay up, or be regulated by the law or industry groups.

I don't think most people would see the problem with that push notification…if, of course, they've previously given the store permission to text them with such offers. But if we're talking about the store sending you a push notification or texting you because they're able to track you around the mall, and you didn't give them permission, then that's a problem. Same with knowing you're going to go to the mall before you do, which can be done by looking at the data gathered about your trips to the store using a platform like Localytics. Given enough trips to the mall every Saturday, the mall, or your favourite store, can send you a push notification on Friday night telling you about the deals going on specifically when you visit. At some point in the not-too-distant future, those deals could also be customized just for you based on your unique smartphone identification code. The funny thing is that if malls and most retailers weren't using Point of Sale software and hardware from the Stone Age, this is something you would have already experienced by now. Don't worry. It's coming real soon.

The mall or store might have assumed you gave them permission to do all this when you gave them your phone number once upon a time while checking out. But you didn't know what it was they were going to do with it. I mean, when those nice people at Yankee Candle or DSW ask you for your phone number, do you ever press them as to why they need it in the first place? Did you know you can say no to them? Maybe it was implied in giving them your number that they can send you stuff, but this is where the issue of clarity comes back into the picture. It's not just the tech companies who are being deliberately vague about collecting and utilizing your data anymore. This book took a specific focus on Internet-enabled devices you own, but the reality is that soon everything around us is going to be wired and talking to each other, so this lack of explanation and clarity from all parties is deeply troubling. It's in a company's best interest not to tell you what's going on. Remember: if you think the Internet is magic, and so are words like 'algorithm', then it's easier for tech companies and other parties to continue being creepy without much supervision or regulation. (This is why shows like *Wisdom of the Crowd* piss me off. Algorithms and tech companies are not magic. Neither is Jeremy Piven.)

Here's the good news. We can always do something about the phone tracking, and it's actually a dead simple thing to do: turn off your smartphone's Wi-Fi and Bluetooth before you get to the store. If those settings aren't activated, you can't be tracked, at least not through your smartphone. To be even more on the safe side, don't tell shops your phone number or email address when they ask (unless you really want those coupons).

One last thing, and this is something I've been experimenting with over the past year: you could just ditch your smartphone. I know. Scandal! But if you keep a disposable phone in your car for emergencies, then, cameras aside, there are really few ways for anyone to track you doing anything. Whatever you choose to do, the unfortunate reality is that big companies who own retail stores are letting the wrong people push them in dumb directions. It's not their customers clamouring to be tracked; it's their shareholders, their upper management, and the tech companies looking to sell their wares to these companies that are pushing for it. Not much you and I can do about that either, but there may be a light at the end of the tunnel: if people stop going to those stores because they're aware of these practices, those upper management types may find themselves out of work, those tech companies without a deal, and those shareholders… OK, you're stuck with those people, but maybe they'll learn a valuable lesson there, too. We have more power than we think; we just have to use it.

CHAPTER SUMMARY

➤ I included this chapter because I didn't want to talk about privacy issues involving only your Internet-enabled devices. The reality is that the issue is much larger, and the practice of being creepy about collecting and utilizing your data bleeds heavily into places you may not expect. Put another way, this chapter is a small sleight of hand. In the immediate future, we have to deal with Google, Amazon, Facebook, Apple, and Microsoft collecting and selling your data and doing other things with it. In the next decade, though, that issue is going to expand to cities, buildings, and stores doing the same thing the tech companies are doing with your data.

➤ Although there's not much you can do about the increasing number of cameras and sensors all around you, one good trick before heading to the mall or store is to turn your phone's location settings, Bluetooth, and Wi-Fi off before going to shop. It may sound like a major inconvenience, but you do have the option available to you.

CHAPTER TEN

STEALING YOUR STUFF

Since we looked one hundred years into the past to see how this privacy thing got started, it's worth taking a peek into the future as well. Not a hundred years into the future, mind you, but definitely over the next decade or so. The good news? By looking at the past, we already know how the future is going to play out. But, before we get there, we need to make a quick stop to talk about hackers and a couple of other things I had on my checklist.

When the contents of this particular chapter were discussed, I had intended to talk to you about LulzSec and Anonymous, but, going into 2018, these are not really topical subjects. So, I'm just going to acknowledge that whole deal here quickly before moving on. Some could argue that Anonymous was never really important at all, but I'm not going to go anywhere near that argument. That's because what gave groups like them power is the lax attitude many companies have toward data security.

That, and the fact that people are still really awful at creating and safeguarding their passwords, is one of our biggest issues moving into the future. The incompetence and laziness on the part of companies to secure our data from criminals. Not that we're immune to this incompetence. I'm looking at you, person who used 'password' as the password for their Netflix account. Remember that big Sony Pictures hack that was committed, potentially, by a state-backed group of hackers from North Korea? Regardless who was responsible for the hack, it doesn't matter for our purposes: Sony employees had a file called 'Passwords' and you can guess what was in it. (Spoiler alert: it was passwords.) So, whoever was behind the initial data breach was able to do way more damage than anticipated when they discovered that file. Which is kind of amazing when you think about it! This is the digital equivalent of going to rob a bank and finding that the people in charge of security left the vault open for you. As dangerous as the media wants you to think hackers are, don't forget about those lazy security measures, or that no one wants to spend money updating security software. As sophisticated and inexpensive as hacking tools are getting today, this is the reason hackers can do so much damage in the first place. That's why we need to push for heavy fines, and maybe even jail time in some cases, for companies that don't take protecting your data seriously. I don't want to see anyone go to jail, but if there are zero consequences for a massive data breach like we saw with Yahoo! and Equifax, then we're going to continue seeing more events like this happening in the future. Funny thing about the

Sony hack: Sony had just spent a lot of time and money upgrading their security infrastructure—or so they claimed after the hack anyway—but you figure that if the company was so concerned about securing their files, they wouldn't have had an easily accessible folder called 'Passwords' just sitting there for someone to find it.

To discuss yet another example, it wasn't too long ago that the director of the CIA's personal emails were being published by Wikileaks. (We're going to skip over the whole 'But what about Hillary's emails?' thing.) How did Wikileaks get this information from the CIA director? The person responsible for providing that information to Wikileaks used good old-fashioned social engineering—calling and pretending to be someone else: in this case, a Verizon employee—to get the email password. Again, the hacker didn't do anything sophisticated here. Clever, sure, but this Mr. Robot 'magic evil hacker' image we have in the media is bogus. Most hackers I know aren't looking to fuck with you, but like any profession, there are great people and assholes to be found among them. It's the assholes, often the minority of that group, that give everyone else a bad name. It's sort of how most priests are decent people you can leave your kids around…

This is just another great example of companies being lax and people being careless about protecting their data. With two-factor authentication enabled, the hacker shouldn't have been able to access the CIA director's email account at all.

I was also supposed to talk to you about Wikileaks, but the fact is Julian Assange is very good at getting publicity for himself, and that's about it. He hasn't really done much beyond release what other people have given to him, and if not for major media outlets going through the files that were put out by Wikileaks, no one would know what they were putting out into the world. So, forget that guy, is what I'm saying.

I mentioned elsewhere that Tor is an excellent tool you should use to help cover your tracks when you browse the Internet, but let it be said that if you're doing something bad, or something you probably shouldn't be doing, you will be found. Tor is commonly used to share information with Wikileaks, which has brought it to the attention of many security organizations. This goes into the whole 'The Internet is Magic' line of thinking I like to talk about, where we think the stuff we use online is flawless and the companies who provide it to us can do no wrong. Yes, people still believe that. And some of those people might think, 'If I use Tor, I'm anonymous' Well, yes, but what about all the stuff you do on your computer when you're not using Tor? All it takes is one little slip and your anonymity, together with any benefit you enjoyed from using Tor, goes right out the window.

And Bitcoin? Other cryptocurrencies? I'm moderately excited about them, but at the time of this writing, I don't think there's much to say just yet. At least from a non-technical point of view. The software could be (and in many cases is being) rolled out to better protect people's data, which is terrific, but I don't think anyone wants to hear me drone on about ledgers and whether your Dogecoin is still worth anything—at least until the field is more developed.

Which brings me to the last item I wanted to cover before we got to the main course. That's the Deep Web (not to be confused with the Dark Web, which is not the same thing). You use the Deep Web ALL the time. In its most basic sense, it's a term that refers to things not easily found via a search engine. That's all the Deep Web is. So, for example, I'm writing this chapter in a Google Doc, which can't be accessed unless I give the link to someone, or share the document publicly. This doc lives on the Deep Web. The Dark Web (or Darkweb) is a tiny pocket of the Deep Web. And you'll be pleased to know that, according to the Tor Project, fewer than three percent of people who use Tor (which is required to access the Dark Web) actually do access the Dark Web, and only a fraction of those people participate in criminal activities. Take that, lazy TV show writers!

What happens when my data's stolen?

This is the question we're all going to have to face in the future. We've established in this book that your data has immense value. Tech companies and their business partners will stop at nothing, even if it means being creepy. But like nearly anything that has value, your data is being lusted after by far more than just them. Case in point: a week after I was approached to write this book, I had a letter on my desk from Experian informing me that an 'unauthorized party' had gotten into their servers. As a result, my information, along with numerous other T-Mobile customers, who Experian had run credit checks on behalf of, had been stolen. This includes my date of birth, Social Security Number, name, address, and Driver's

License information. This isn't the first time I've received a letter like this. In fact, over the past few years in the United States, if you're a Target or Home Depot customer, or happen to have your insurance provided by one of the many brands of Anthem Inc., then you've gotten one of these letters too. And if you're in the United Kingdom, do I have to say anything more than: TalkTalk?

If you're wondering what you can do about any of this, the answer can be found, again, in the EU's GDPR regulations. These issues involving your data are often the result of unregulated security practices. Under GDPR, these companies can be fined for lax data security. We need consequences here in the US, too. Otherwise the result is what you see on Wall Street, where they're back to doing the same stuff now that they were doing to cause The Great Recession. No consequences means no change.

Businesses are not your friend. The days of my grandfather's store are long gone. Small businesses aside, the large companies that dominate our lives are always going to err on the side of saving money instead of spending it. And, less often occurring, but no less important, is the increasing amount of sophistication on the part of the few asshole hackers who access your data. They're going to wisely take advantage of dumb companies.

Criminals you can, and in this case should, punish—greedy and incompetent corporations included. The only difference is, we have laws on the books to go after criminal hackers. Ryan Collins, who may or may not have been one of the hackers involved with the leaked nude celebrity photos I told you about previously, was sentenced to eighteen months in prison for phishing and trying out other methods to access the photos and other information. One of those methods involved using a program—one that the Apple patch would have stopped—to download all the contents from the iCloud accounts he targeted. Collins went to jail, and everyone forgot about Apple's little oopsy and Reddit benefitting from hosting those photos.

Additionally, and this might sound ridiculous, because I do take hackers seriously, you would be surprised by how often the answer to the question of 'Who hacked Company X' is 'It was a former employee.' Just ask Morgan Stanley. I encourage you the next time you hear about some huge data breach, to dig deep into the story. Then, as you do so, you should take a drink every time you read the phrase, 'ex-employee suspected'

If you look real close at most big security breaches, more often than not you'll find that an angry ex-employee or lax security on the company's part is at fault, not an 'evil hacker' type. Initial reports might say it was a hacker, but if you keep up with the story, you'll often see it change from 'hacker' to 'hacker plus bad security' to 'ex-employee' And if it's not? Would you believe that a lot of these huge security breaches occur through some good old-fashioned phishing? With Home Depot, the hackers were able to install invasive software by using stolen login credentials that belonged to an outside vendor who lacked tight security protocols. This, by the way, is similar to what happened with Target, where the hackers were able to get into the Target system via an HVAC company that had an unusually robust amount of access to Target's servers. How'd they get the HVAC company's information? Good old-fashioned phishing.

You probably know what phishing is, even if you might not know the name. It's when you get an email that looks like it belongs to a friend or service you use, asking you to log in to your account. Sometimes these emails even come with a link to a website that looks like the website of a service you use, but actually isn't. So instead of SheetRock.com you might see a phishing email sent from SheetRock.co or SheetRockinc.com. If you don't catch that these websites are decoys, you may log in to what you think is your account, as a phishing email instructs, and give these decoy services access to your data—thus allowing the hackers operating the decoy website to steal your credentials. To add insult to injury, for weeks after the massive Equifax data breach in the fall of 2017, people were being redirected, by Equifax, to sites that had no relation to Equifax whatsoever, and those sites were collecting data. In a rare bit of good news: some of those sites were set up by a good Samaritan developer who told *The Verge* he set up the pages to point out to Equifax how dangerous it was to send customers to sites unrelated to their company since it was so easy for scammers to set up sites that were similar and could actually steal data.

You know why people are so susceptible to phishing? What I've learned from my own usability tests as well as from other start-ups who have done similar tests is this: drunk people browse the Web the same way sober people do. In other words, most people don't really stop to think when using the Web or an app. We just click or tap mindlessly away. (We're busy, remember?) So, if you're not thinking, and you get an email from PayPal, or any other service provider you're connected to, saying you need to log in, and you're distracted by other stuff, you're just going to click. And no one will be the wiser until people in your address book start getting hit with a wall of spam sent from 'you'.

What I recommend you do, if you ever fall victim to one of these emails, is this:

One, change your password. Then, sign up for a credit monitoring service. I use the one Mint.com offers because I already use their platform for other things, but there are plenty of choices out there, including Experian's now ironically-named ProtectMyID.

Two, get yourself a credit report to keep an eye on things. I get a free credit report each year from AnnualCreditReport.com.

What can criminals do with your data?

Criminals can do almost anything with your data. From really annoying things like opening up a credit card in your name, to really scary like going to jail under your identity. That means that their jail time will show up on your records whenever someone does a background check. Good luck explaining to your next boss why you did prison time as a burglar during the same period of time you claimed to be in college.

According to a 2014 report by the RAND corporation, your data, and the selling of it by criminals, is more profitable than the illegal drug trade. The more information a criminal has on you, the more money they can make by selling it. And the more information a criminal has, the more information they can get. Put another way: criminals can use the data they already have on you to get even more of it. The idea is that, the data they have gives them the information needed to crack your more secure accounts.

When you enter your password on certain websites the only concern is that it be the right one. Other websites, however, more sophisticated ones, are simultaneously looking at other elements you enter to make sure you are who you say you are. For example, on the Verizon website, when I log in to pay my bill, I see a security picture in addition to being asked to enter my password and security question. But if I'm a criminal and I just have your password, then when I try to enter into sites with that extra step (the picture and security question), I can't. By collecting more data about you though, I can easily guess your security question's answer, which would help me access your account. In fact, you may have used the same security question and answer for another site I already broke into as you. One thing gives me access to more things. So, if your data is stolen, the effects can be cumulative. I can make more money from that data as a criminal by obtaining more and more of it, and the more I have, the more I can break into other services you use. So, if you hear about one of these data breaches and you go, "It'll be fine. They just have my driver's license number", there is still reason to be worried and vigilant, since that one bit of data will give them access to even more data. (A recurring theme in this book: the answer is for less data to be collected, not more, in order to provide you with a service.)

Just because there's nothing we can do to stop our

information from being accessed, it doesn't mean we should be lax about protecting it. The mind-set should be to minimize your potential for harm. You should take the management of your email password (and your other passwords, too, for that matter) very seriously. Your email primarily, since it's the gateway hackers most often use to get access to your other data. So, make sure you change your password every year, and make sure not to click on things that look suspicious. The filters of email providers are getting more sophisticated every day, but they don't at all account for human error, and none of us are perfect.

What to know about your rights

If you're under the age of thirteen and reside in the United States, you enjoy a lot of protection under the Child Online Protection Act and other pieces of legislation. If you're older, however, things start to get a little wonky. This is partly the result of the Constitution not explicitly stating anywhere that you have a right to privacy (although it's implicitly stated in several amendments in the Bill of Rights), and partly the result of the Supreme Court saying you do have a right to privacy, but then in large part the failure of what laws we do have on the books coming out of those court decisions, and other legislation that just hasn't caught up to the age we live in.

To summarize: if you're under thirteen, or a celebrity, you have certain protections in place. Thirteen-year-olds because they're too young to know any better, and celebrities because their image and likeness have value. If you're older than that, and significantly less famous than Gal Gadot, then a lot of it boils down to, yes, you're protected in theory, but sorry, the state doesn't cover you. This is because the federal government has been a bit slow…well, to do much of anything. That's how governments work. Slowly. This is also why I'm personally an advocate of the states taking up the mantle of protecting your privacy and updating their legislation to give you better access and control over who has your information, how long they'll have your information for, and what they're going to be doing with it. Your state representative is going to get back to you much faster than your federal representative. While we're at it, we should be talking compensation as well with your state officials. It's your data. As I've asked before: why aren't you getting anything from its commercial use? And for those of you who are opposed to the government doing anything here, even on the state level, I am totally fine with a non-profit independent organization stepping in to fill the void, if that means getting these concessions from the tech and advertising companies. Let's just get it fixed.

The good news if you happen not to be a celebrity or under thirteen years of age, is that there are many organizations and people working to address the gaps in the law that don't protect your privacy and data from being abused by tech companies and other parties. The following organizations have your back, and deserve your support:

EPIC: The Electronic Privacy Information Center
EFF: The Electronic Frontier Foundation
The Privacy Coalition
ACLU: The American Civil Liberties Union
US-CERT: The United States Computer Emergency

Readiness Team

And yes, the FTC: The Federal Trade Commission

CHAPTER SUMMARY

➤ Don't blame the hackers. There are always going to be people who are looking to screw you over if given the opportunity. It's up to you to be vigilant, watch what you're clicking or tapping on, and push for your state to create better regulations on the use (and abuse) of your data. Lax security policies on the part of large corporations because they don't want to protect your data or spend the money to do so should be wholly unacceptable.

➤ When in doubt about a large security breach or hack, the smart money is almost always on a disgruntled former employee having done it.

CHAPTER ELEVEN

THEN AGAIN, SO WHAT?

If you want to be successful in life, there's no real trick to it. You just have to be able to see things from other people's perspectives. So, I'm going to touch on some possible counterpoints to the information in this book as we wrap up our time together.

In a lot of ways, the debate involving privacy and the use and misuse of your data mirrors the debate involving climate change. Most people would agree (provided you say 'climate change' and not 'global warming') that climate change is a major issue that needs to be addressed. But then they assume that, first, there's nothing they can do about it, and, second, that climate change won't affect them in their lifetime, so they go about their business and just don't think about it. You can see this solipsism played out in a short video Bill Nye did with *National Geographic*. It's the one where he's showing how Miami will be underwater because of rising sea levels due to climate change, and then the video cuts to Bill Nye talking to a Miami resident who thinks he'll be unaffected by climate change…because he lives in Miami.

Put another way, the response to the abuse and use of someone's private data can best be summed up in two simple words: So what! But there are a lot of different reasons why people use those words. I'm going to give you three of the most important and common ones to think about it.

"So what! If Facebook tracks my location when I'm not even logged into their app, it makes no difference in my life."

"So what! There's nothing I can do to stop those huge tech giants from being creepy with my data. For every case of shadiness we know about, there's probably a ton more we don't hear about because the company isn't big enough to be called out for doing it. Besides, these companies are entertaining me. It's not like they're forcing me to use them. I want to use their offerings."

"So what! If the government knows everything there is to know about me, why should it be any different for a company, especially when they use that data to make my life easier? We live in times when I can have donuts delivered to my house, by drone, before I know I even want them. What a time to be alive!"

If we're being honest, there's no great response to these points. That's the biggest failure of most books on privacy. They just go on and on and on, beating you to death with their politics as an answer to these questions. I honestly just don't have a good answer beyond what I've said in the previous chapters. It's exceptionally hard to get people to think about the future and the consequences of their actions when those consequences may not even culminate for years to come. I think you should be compensated for the sale of your data, and these companies should be responsible for the times they mess up and leak your info. They should be fined and maybe even some people must face jail. I also think these companies need to take the initiative to better inform you of how they use your data, and give you more control over that. And, if they don't, then a regulatory body or a state agency needs to get involved to make them do so. Now, after the Equifax breach, all bets are off and everyone's data is out there. So, if we don't take this seriously now, when will we? Maybe never. Then what? You have to ask yourself what kind of world you want to live in. Remember that Donald Trump got elected President, not because of Russian interference in the election, but because of voter apathy. As *The Washington Post* reported, close to 100 million people didn't come out to vote. That's more than the number of people who voted for each of the respective candidates. The people who did not vote, for whatever reason, decided, through inertia, that Trump was an acceptable candidate. It might sound extreme to say this, but we're dealing with a similar situation when it comes to your data and the ramifications of it being collected by companies that I outlined in this book. Left to their own devices, the tech companies and members of the advertising industry will make themselves rich, jobs will be wiped out through the utilization of that data and automation, billions of dollars in taxes (that we badly need) will go unpaid, and algorithms will be used to discriminate against you in ways you won't even hear about until it's too late.

Either you think the collection and abuse of your private data is a problem, or you don't. If you don't, there isn't any reason to care about it because it (seemingly) doesn't affect your day to day life. I get it. We all have shit to do. I can certainly make an emotional appeal to you. That your right to privacy, while not guaranteed in the Constitution explicitly, is heavily implied within its first ten amendments and has been further defended by the Supreme Court. I can also say to you that your credit score, just as one example, could be determined in part by your Twitter profile.

What I've just laid out for you throughout this book is why it's so difficult for anything to get done about this issue. Why haven't our laws been strengthened to prevent the abuse of our private data? Because a lot of this argument has yet to be framed in such a way as to cause a strong emotional reaction to it. Think: boring words, which is what we have currently, versus that wildly successful but really depressing Sarah McLachlan commercial that comes on for the ASPCA. One doesn't provoke an action, and the other does. It's up to you reading this book to decide which side of the fence you want to be on. I know that this stuff matters, even if I don't regularly see it, so I want to do something about it now, while there's still time to do so.

Last words

I wish I had something profound here to say about privacy, but all I have is that there's no such thing as privacy anymore. Not since 1917. So, we're at that stage where we need to decide what to do, and at the moment we're letting greedy tech companies and advertising companies move the discussion forward.

I don't profess to speak for the advertising industry, but I've been around it long enough to echo what many of us like to say in the dark corners of the office when the clients aren't listening. If the client thinks Facebook advertising is wonderful, then the agency is going to agree with the client and spend millions of dollars on Facebook advertising. As living advertising legend Bob Hoffman told me, "In marketing today, it is better to be wrong within the normal range than right outside the normal range. Being critical of the value of advertising on Facebook and Google is outside the normal range." So, if you read through this book and you go, why does the advertising industry put so much money into the products of creepy companies and questionable data, it's not because they're evil. It's because someone told them it was a good idea, and that someone was probably writing their checks. That's the truth in America. Our economy sucks and we'll do whatever it takes to get paid, up to and including working for dumb companies and telling them what a great idea tracking their customers to the bathroom in their own home is.

When push comes to shove, the economic incentives are not at all in your favour to make a change. The ad industry and tech companies are going to lobby real hard to make sure a Privacy Bill of Rights on the federal level never comes into existence. They successfully stopped the Obama administration at virtually every turn on that front. (And the Obama administration, to their own detriment, also had more than a few opportunities to crack down on Google and Facebook through the FTC and the Department of Justice—and opted not to do so. So, they're not exactly blameless here either.)

That's not a great way to end a book. So, I've put together some good news to share with you: Apple, for all its faults, made a change to the Safari Browser in iOS 11. This change will severely limit the amount of data an advertiser can extract from you after 30 days, using first-party cookies. The advertising industry, naturally, flipped out. Google's Chrome browser will also be cracking down on advertising online, but not the tracking aspects of it. Just the shitty aspects, like when you go to a site to read a dumb listicle and an auto-playing ad kicks on, followed by an advertisement that takes over the entire home screen, promoting something like lottery tickets. The tools to protect yourself and your data are also getting better. Virtual Private Networks (VPNs) are less and less expensive and tedious to install on your personal computers and mobile devices. You can use the Signal app—endorsed by Edward Snowden, no less—to send secure messages to other Signal users, and breathe easily knowing that the people behind Signal don't store any of the data being sent over the app. So, it's not like the latest version of iOS or the current versions of Android where the keyboard and operating system are keeping track of what you're sending, and then sharing it with the NSA and pretty much everyone else they feel like, in order to make 'suggestions' on what you should type next. Signal is the complete opposite of that, and it's convenient and easy to use. For those of you using Android on your phone, or a laptop in general, you can also use the Tor browser and related software (which can be found online at TorProject.org) to more securely browse and utilize the Internet on your devices. And, of course, you can always do little things like clear out your cookies and history after each browsing session, too. I have Firefox set up to do that every time I close it out, so I don't have to keep reminding myself to make that happen. So, the good news again: there are little things you can do to protect yourself right now.

Some states are also showing initiative to protect you, in light of the federal government not being able to accomplish much of anything. It's hard for me to describe anything the federal government has gotten done in the time that I've been of voting age, aside from fighting and obstructing each other, and that's true for Democrats as well as Republicans. But, some states like Washington do have a section on privacy written into their state constitution. I know no one likes a hodgepodge of rules and regulations, but it's not the worst thing to ask your state representatives to consider passing a privacy bill of rights to help protect your data and your privacy in general. Especially now, as we're approaching so many Internet-connected devices out there that you would never think are collecting data about you, but totally are. Like the Roomba. Yes. The Roomba. In the summer of 2017, a brief firestorm ignited after the CEO of the company iRobot, Colin Angle, mentioned his plans for the Roomba to map your home and potentially provide that data to data brokers or companies like Amazon and Google. After the firestorm, the company mentioned that customers would be given the choice to opt in to have their homes mapped. Sound familiar, though? Company does something creepy, people freak out about it, company backs off, and then when they get a chance later, they go right back to doing it. Making people 'opt in' through the Terms of Service is especially unacceptable, and it's the go-to tactic these days. But if you live in a state like New York, and the Attorney General's office has the capability to take action against iRobot because the state has some quality privacy laws on the books, you'd better believe they'll think twice about being creepy again. And, if you don't live in a state that has a privacy bill of rights, having the New York Attorney General's office tackle the issue may cause your own state's AG to join the fray. We've seen that before with things like the Trump administration's travel ban, where AGs across the country teamed up to attack it. It's up to us to make that happen. Unlike on the federal level, we can get things done on the state level. I've seen it. I formed a Political Action Committee and a not-for-profit to support a citizens' group where my parents live. It took years, but they won their battle by organizing and making their voices heard. (10,000 people in the area also would have backed me for Congress. So...grassroots organizing may sound lame and ineffective, but it works.)

On the federal level, that approach doesn't really work, but in state elections (and, in some instances, congressional races), every vote and voice does indeed matter. And if you're not fired up to vote after the last presidential election, I don't know what to tell you. Just remember that hundred million number the next time Trump says or does something insane. Change is possible. The challenge is getting everyone up off the couch and outside to interact with their fellow humans in making their state a better place for everyone. By reading this book, you're already halfway there. Now the other half is the fun part of organizing your friends and neighbours, and calling on your state politicians to take action. I've said this before in interviews on this subject, but even if the state fails in its quest to get the tech companies and data brokers to change, the very threat of change may be enough to get the data industries to regulate themselves, in much the same way as the video game industry did in the 1990s and Microsoft did after the Department of Justice went after them in the early noughts.

By the way, something I didn't delve into is the state government and federal government themselves collecting far more data than they need to in order to process services for you. Although there are laws, like FERPA and HIPAA, that protect your privacy in very specific instances (like if you're a college student or a patient accessing medical care), there's no blanket privacy protection law out there to protect you. That's something a privacy bill of rights can do if one was to be created where you live. Many people worry about identity theft, and one way to reduce (if not eliminate) the possibility of that is by restricting how much information is collected about you in the first place. I talked a lot about private companies and businesses doing that to you, but the same is also true of your government. Limiting the amount of over-sharing that goes on doesn't hurt anyone, and protects you in the process, so it's really hard to be against that.

If you're wondering whether I have a specific bill of rights in mind, or things I'd like to see in it, the answer is no, I don't. Not beyond what's suggested here in this book. But I can tell you two things I want that I hope I can sell you on, since I've been hitting on them throughout our time together. The first is that I personally don't care if some company I've never heard of has over 10,000 data points about me, ranging from my porn fetish to the fact that I drive an old Subaru Forester. But I sure as shit would like to make some profit from that exchange. Wouldn't you? I have no problem selling my data—it's my data to sell. My data, my choice. Why don't I have any option at all here to cash in on this? If I go to Facebook, or to some website that belongs to a giant ad network like Oath, then Oath gets to collect my data and use it to tell brands and agencies that they have the 'secret sauce' needed to advertise to me. Oath makes a ton of cash, and I get nothing. There's something about that which just eats away at my soul. If it was up to me, advertisers should pay me for my data in exchange for the right to advertise to me. As for Facebook—which would be harmed in that arrangement since the advertisers no longer need them—I would happily pay for an advertisement-free Facebook experience, as long as the data they collected at that point was only to provide me with a better service and they did nothing more with it. Same with Twitter. They blew more than a few chances to have people pay for an upgraded experience, but they just can't seem to get their act together. Instead, we don't get these options. We get bad user experiences across the Internet and Web. As one Reddit user on the subreddit /r/

advertising described our collective user experience, in answering the question of why advertisers are hated:

"Check out my blog for the 6 things you didn't know about advertisers, the 4th one will really get your jimmies rustled. Want more from me in your inbox, like and subscribe, don't forget to click the bell. Without your support we will go out of business; please share your email address to receive special offers right to your inbox each day. Oh, we noticed you're using an ad blocker, disable it to view all our great content. Hey, we're going to use your CPU cycles to mine bitcoins since you block all our ads. Hey, we see you're trying to leave, don't forget to sign up for our hourly updates on more BS you don't care about. Please, please be our friend, our website is dying.

Oh, we see you're on mobile, here's an ad banner, a modal with a newsletter signup form, a banner to acknowledge we use cookies (because who doesn't), and wait for it…there it is, an auto-playing review video we just made about popsicle sticks. Hey, we noticed you just purchased a washing machine, looks like you're interested in washing machines, here's a banner ad about washing machines in case you have buyer's remorse and return the one you just purchased or something. Hey, we geo-tracked you as visiting your grandma during thanksgiving, this must mean you're interested in our local uni-cycle shop, click here for our current promotions and to sign up for our weekly newsletter packed full of tips and tricks. Did you know? We have a YouTube channel featuring a long intro with dance music made in PowerPoint about our uni-cycles. Washing machines. And on. And on."

What I get, what we all get, is bullshit. No value. And I

think that has to change. If we give something, we should get something. If I pay for an advertisement-free and non-creepy experience, that's what I should get. If you're going to gobble up my data and provide it to third parties for a cool billion dollars, I should get a cut of that. If you're going to wipe out jobs in the name of being efficient, you should be paying the billions of dollars in taxes that you owe so those unemployed people can be trained for new jobs. Right now, we're living in a world where only one side benefits, and aren't you just getting a little tired of that sort of arrangement? Put another way: never forget that a lot of these companies are just repositories for your stuff. Without your stuff, there would be no business or profit for them to speak of. Facebook is nothing without you.

Given the current state of the global economy, the rising tide of automation, and all these other nightmare scenarios that seem to be increasingly playing out on a daily basis, the least I think we can do is give us all some cold hard cash in exchange for our data. You know how everyone seems to be talking about a universal basic income, but they don't know where the money will come from to fund it—well, shit, here's your solution! Let the ad and tech industries pay people an annual license fee in exchange for their data. There are a lot of ways for us to slice this pizza and change the way things are; we just have to stop talking about it and start doing it.

The final thing I want to sell you on is something we touched on earlier in the book. This Terms of Service thing. I'm no lawyer, but many lawyers would describe a Terms of Service agreement as a 'contract by adhesion'. Essentially, it's an agreement between two parties where one party has no real choice in the matter. It's a 'take it or leave it proposition': you either agree, or you don't get to use and enjoy the thing with that Terms of Service contract. That's essentially the situation we have with the Terms of Service on all your devices and platforms (at least outside of the European Union), and that's not acceptable. You know what that gets called in the education field these days? Bullying. What we should fight for, if we're going to fight for anything, is making the collection and use of our data more explicit and clear. Who is getting your data? What are they going to do with it? How long will they have access to your data? These three questions should not take nearly 6,000 words in legalese to answer. Watch, I'll prove it to you. Everyone reading this book will get a free PDF copy of my last book, *Social Media Is Bullshit*, if they text me at 646-331-8341 with the word 'Sheetrock'. I'm totally serious. Text me with that word, and I will text you back with the .pdf. It won't be a bot or any kind of automated response. It'll be me. Now, who is getting your data (your phone number) in this case? I am. What am I going to do with it? Nothing, because I'm kind of lazy and have no patience at all to work on something like a newsletter (although email newsletters are incredibly valuable, if often abused, as a marketing channel). I just don't have the attention span to bother you with shit on a regular basis. Who is the data going to be shared with? No one. I'll send you a text, hit the delete button, and never think about it again. See? Nice, simple, and clear, answering the questions of who gets your data, what they're going to use it for, and how long they'll have it. And I even rambled in there. So: regardless of what form this more explicit opt-in looks like, you and I both know that there are far better ways to exchange information with each other than the busted Terms of Service model that has dominated the Web virtually since its beginnings. You should not be expected to have a college degree to understand what some company is doing with all the information it's collecting on you. Aside from compensating you, the least they can do is give you more control over what's being collected and how, in clear and specific terms. And if they don't want to do it? It's time for the state government or an independent organization to step in and fight the good fight on your behalf.

If you liked this book email me here and let me know: bj@bjmendelson.com. Or text me at 646-331-8341. As long as you learned something and now better understand what's going on with your data and privacy as it relates to the Internet, then I'd like to think I've accomplished the job I was asked to do. Let's just hope I don't almost die again between books, and I'll see you with the next one.

"Privacy may actually be an anomaly."

—Vint Cerf

BIBLIOGRAPHY & FURTHER READING

"5 Things You Need to Know About Climate Change." National Geographic Channel. July 28, 2016. Accessed October 12, 2017. http://channel.nationalgeographic.com/explorer/videos/5-things-you-need-to-know-about-climate-change/?utm_source=Facebook&utm_medium=Social&utm_content=link_fb20151012ch-climatevid&utm_campaign=Content&sf13978903=1.

America, Jun 05 2013 North. "The 'Social' Credit Score: Separating the Data from the Noise." Knowledge@Wharton. June 5, 2013. Accessed October 12, 2017. http://knowledge.wharton.upenn.edu/article/the-social-credit-score-separating-the-data-from-the-noise/.

Angwin, Julia, and Steve Stecklow. "'Scrapers' Dig Deep for Data on Web." The Wall Street Journal. October 12, 2010. Accessed October 06, 2017. http://www.wsj.com/articles/SB10001424052748703358504575544381288117888.

Arrington, Michael. "Octazen: What The Heck Did Facebook Just Buy Exactly, And Why?" TechCrunch. February 19, 2010. Accessed October 06, 2017. https://techcrunch.com/2010/02/19/octazen-what-the-heck-did-facebook-just-buy-exactly-and-why/.

"Art. 17 GDPR – Right to Erasure ('right to Be Forgotten')." General Data Protection Regulation (GDPR). Accessed October 14, 2017. https://gdpr-info.eu/art-17-gdpr/.

Barnett, Michael. "Marketers Call for 'clear and Consistent' Guidance on GDPR." Marketing Week. September 25, 2017. Accessed October 14, 2017. https://www.marketingweek.com/2017/05/25/gdpr/.

Benes, Ross. "'Everyone Has Been Wary': Inside the Adblock Plus 'acceptable Ads' Committee." Digiday. March 17, 2017. Accessed October 04, 2017. https://digiday.com/media/adblock-committee/.

Biddle, Sam, and Nitasha Tiku. "Did Path Cheat Its Way to The Top?" Gawker. June 13, 2013. Accessed October 06, 2017. http://valleywag.gawker.com/did-path-cheat-its-way-to-the-top-494127268.

Biddle, Sam. "Stop Using Unroll.me, Right Now. It Sold Your Data to Uber." The Intercept. April 24, 2017. Accessed October 14, 2017. https://theintercept.com/2017/04/24/stop-using-unroll-me-right-now-it-sold-your-data-to-uber/.

Blue, Violet. "What If Russian Voter Hacks Were Just Part of Its Facebook Ad Campaign?" Engadget. October 06, 2017. Accessed October 06, 2017. https://www.engadget.com/2017/10/06/russian-voter-hacks-support-facebook-ad-campaign/.

Brooks, Chad. "Shoppers Still Prefer In-Store Over Online Shopping." Business News Daily. February 10, 2015. Accessed October 12, 2017. http://www.businessnewsdaily.com/7756-online-shopping-preferences.html.

Catsoulis, Jeannette. "Narrow Space in Society, If Any, for Anonymity." The New York Times. July 11, 2013. Accessed October 05, 2017. http://www.nytimes.com/2013/07/12/movies/terms-and-conditions-may-apply-details-digital-age-loss-of-privacy.html?_r=0.

"The Center for Responsive Politics." OpenSecrets.org. Accessed October 05, 2017. http://www.opensecrets.org/orgs/summary.php?id=D000067823.

Chadha, Rahul. "Consumers Concerned About IoT Device Hacking." EMarketer. October 23, 2017. Accessed October 23, 2017. https://www.emarketer.com/Article/Consumers-Concerned-About-IoT-Device-Hacking/1016652?ecid=NL1001.

Conrady, Stacy. "How Does Google Maps Know Where Traffic Is?" Mental Floss. April 03, 2017. Accessed October 12, 2017. http://mentalfloss.com/article/92958/how-does-google-maps-know-where-traffic.

Cook, James. "There Is a Secret 'success Rate' Hidden in All Your Tinder Photos." Business Insider. March 09, 2017. Accessed October 14, 2017. http://www.businessinsider.com/tinder-secret-success-rate-photos-right-swipe-percentage-2017-3.

Cox, Kate. "New, Updated Foursquare Is Always Watching You... Even When You Aren't Running Foursquare."

Consumerist. September 27, 2016. Accessed October 11, 2017. http://consumerist.com/2014/08/07/new-updated-foursquare-is-always-watching-you-even-when-you-arent-running-foursquare/.

"Crunchbase: Path." Path. Accessed October 10, 2017. https://www.crunchbase.com/organization/path.

Davies, Chris. "Nest Google Privacy Row Resumes as Thermostat Hacked." SlashGear. June 24, 2014. Accessed October 06, 2017. http://www.slashgear.com/nest-google-privacy-row-resumes-as-thermostat-hacked-24334930/.

Davies, Jessica. "Facebook Video Ad Viewability Rates Are as Low as 20 Percent, Agencies Say." Digiday. June 28, 2017. Accessed October 14, 2017. https://digiday.com/marketing/facebook-video-ad-viewability-rates-low-20-percent-agencies-say/.

Deahl, Dani, and Ashley Carman. "For Weeks, Equifax

Customer Service Has Been Directing Victims to a Fake Phishing Site." The Verge. September 20, 2017. Accessed October 12, 2017. https://www.theverge.com/2017/9/20/16339612/equifax-tweet-wrong-website-phishing-identity-monitoring.

DeNisco, Alison. "Why Ex-employees May Be Your Company's Biggest Cyberthreat." TechRepublic. August 2, 2017. Accessed October 11, 2017. http://www.techrepublic.com/article/why-ex-employees-may-be-your-companys-biggest-cyberthreat/.

Dooley, Roger. "Paper Beats Digital In Many Ways, According To Neuroscience." Forbes. April 14, 2016. Accessed October 14, 2017. https://www.forbes.com/sites/rogerdooley/2015/09/16/paper-vs-digital/#4991b4b333c3.

Downs, Ray. "A Brief History of the US Government Spying on Its Citizens." Vice. June 14, 2013. Accessed October 05, 2017. http://www.vice.com/read/a-brief-history-of-the-united-states-governments-warrentless-spying.

Duportail, Judith. "I Asked Tinder for My Data. It Sent Me 800 Pages of My Deepest, Darkest Secrets." The Guardian. September 26, 2017. Accessed October 14, 2017. https://www.theguardian.com/technology/2017/sep/26/tinder-personal-data-dating-app-messages-hacked-sold.

Fidelman, Mark. "Meet the Growth Hacking Wizard behind Facebook, Twitter and Quora's Astonishing Success." Forbes. October 16, 2013. Accessed October 06, 2017. https://www.forbes.com/sites/markfidelman/2013/10/15/meet-the-growth-hacking-wizard-behind-facebook-twitter-and-quoras-astonishing-success/#468272e748a2.

Friedersdorf, Conor. "82 Years Before Edward Snowden, There Was Herbert O. Yardley." The Atlantic. December 04, 2013. Accessed October 05, 2017. http://www.theatlantic.com/politics/

archive/2013/12/82-years-before-edward-snowden-there-was-herbert-o-yardley/282019/.

Frier, Sarah, and Bill Allison. "Facebook Fought Rules That Could Have Exposed Fake Russian Ads." Bloomberg. com. October 04, 2017. Accessed October 06, 2017. https://www.bloomberg.com/news/articles/2017-10-04/facebook-fought-for-years-to-avoid-political-ad-disclosure-rules.

Frommer, Dan. "Google's Last Dodgeball Employee Leaving To Join Foursquare." Business Insider. August 07, 2009. Accessed October 11, 2017. http://www.businessinsider.com/googles-last-dodgeball-employee-leaving-to-join-foursquare-2009-8.

"FTC Recommends Congress Require the Data Broker Industry to Be More Transparent and Give Consumers Greater Control Over Their Personal Information." Federal Trade Commission. June 19, 2014. Accessed October 06, 2017. https://www.ftc.gov/news-events/press-releases/2014/05/ftc-recommends-congress-require-data-bro-ker-industry-be-more?utm_source=govdelivery.

Gallagher - Oct 20, 2017 3:22 Pm UTC, Sean. "NYPD Can't Get Story Straight on Evidence System Backups." Ars Technica. October 20, 2017. Accessed October 22, 2017. https://arstechnica.com/information-technology/2017/10/nypd-cant-get-story-straight-on-evidence-system-backups/.

Galloway, Scott. The Four: The Hidden DNA of Amazon, Apple, Facebook, and Google. NY, NY: Portfolio/Penguin, 2017.

Galloway, Scott. The Four: The Hidden DNA of Amazon, Apple, Facebook, and Google. NY, NY: Portfolio/Penguin, 2017.

Glaser, April. "Facebook Is Using an "NRA Approach" to Defend Its Creepy Facial Recognition Programs." Slate Magazine. August 04, 2017. Accessed October 14, 2017. http://www.slate.com/blogs/

future_tense/2017/08/04/facebook_is_fighting_biometric_facial_recognition_privacy_laws.html.

Goldman, David. "Rapleaf Is Selling Your Identity." CNNMoney. October 21, 2010. Accessed October 06, 2017. http://money.cnn.com/2010/10/21/technology/rapleaf/index.htm.

Grandoni, Dino. "Instagram Regulations Get Tweaked After Uproar -- But The Worst Part Is Still There." The Huffington Post. December 21, 2012. Accessed October 11, 2017. http://www.huffingtonpost.com/2012/12/21/instagram-regulations_n_2342509.html.

Grauer, Yael. "Hit App Sarahah Quietly Uploads Your Address Book." The Intercept. August 27, 2017. Accessed October 06, 2017. https://theintercept.com/2017/08/27/hit-app-sarahah-quietly-uploads-your-address-book/.

Greenberg, Andy. "Hacked Celeb Pics Made Reddit Enough Cash to Run Its Servers for a Month." Wired. June 03, 2017. Accessed October 14, 2017. https://www.wired.com/2014/09/celeb-pics-reddit-gold/.

Greenwald, Glenn. "NSA Collecting Phone Records of Millions of Verizon Customers Daily." The Guardian. June 06, 2013. Accessed October 05, 2017. http://www.theguardian.com/world/2013/jun/06/nsa-phone-records-verizon-court-order.

Gross, Daniel A. "The US Confiscated Half a Billion Dollars in Private Property During WWI." Smithsonian.com. July 28, 2014. Accessed October 04, 2017. https://www.smithsonianmag.com/history/us-confiscated-half-billion-dollars-private-property-during-wwi-180952144/.

Gye, Hugo. "Google Faces Paying out 'billions of Dollars' after Appeal Court Rules Privacy Campaigners Can Sue over Illegal Data

Gathering with Its Street View Cars." Daily Mail Online. September 11, 2013. Accessed October 11, 2017. http://www.dailymail.co.uk/news/article-2417432/Google-broke-law-harvesting-data-peoples-homes-Street-View-cars.html.

Handley, Lucy. "Businesses Could Lose $16.4 Billion to Online Advertising Fraud in 2017: Report." CNBC. April 13, 2017. Accessed October 14, 2017. https://www.cnbc.com/2017/03/15/businesses-could-lose-164-billion-to-online-advert-fraud-in-2017.html.

Hardwick, Tim. "Fake Chrome Web Browser Extension Unwittingly Installed by 37,000 Users." Mac Rumors. October 10, 2017. Accessed October 10, 2017. https://www.macrumors.com/2017/10/10/fake-chrome-extension-google-web-store/.

Heater, Brian. "IRobot's CEO Defends Roomba Home Mapping as Privacy Concerns arise." TechCrunch. July 25, 2017. Accessed October 12, 2017. https://techcrunch.com/2017/07/25/irobots-ceo-defends-roomba-home-mapping-as-privacy-concerns-arise/.

Heater, Brian. "IRobot's CEO Defends Roomba Home Mapping as Privacy Concerns arise." TechCrunch. July 25, 2017. Accessed October 12, 2017. https://techcrunch.com/2017/07/25/irobots-ceo-defends-roomba-home-mapping-as-privacy-concerns-arise/.

Heine, Christopher. "Rapleaf Agrees to Leave Facebook Alone." ClickZ Rapleaf Agrees to Leave Facebook Alone Comments. November 01, 2010. Accessed October 10, 2017. https://www.clickz.com/rapleaf-agrees-to-leave-facebook-alone/54025/.

Hesseldahl, Arik. "How the US Knew North Korea Was Behind the Sony Hack." Recode. January 18, 2015. Accessed October 12, 2017. https://www.recode.net/2015/1/18/11557884/how-the-u-s-knew-north-korea-was-behind-the-sony-hack.

Hoffman, Bob. "The Data Delusion." The Ad Contrarian. April

3, 2013. Accessed October 06, 2017. http://adcontrarian.blogspot.com/2013/04/the-data-delusion.html.

Hoffman, Bob. "What Every CEO Needs To Know About Online Advertising." The Ad Contrarian. December 8, 2014. Accessed October 14, 2017. http://adcontrarian.blogspot.com/2014/12/what-every-ceo-needs-to-know-about.html.

How Does Facebook Work with Data Providers? | Facebook Help Center | Facebook. Accessed October 06, 2017. https://www.facebook.com/help/494750870625830?helpref=uf_permalink.

"How Retailers Use Smartphones To Track Shoppers In The Store." NPR. June 16, 2014. Accessed October 12, 2017. http://www.npr.org/2014/06/16/322597862/how-retailers-use-smartphones-to-track-shoppers-in-the-store.

Johnston - Jan 16, 2014 12:30 Am UTC, Casey. "What Google Can Really Do with Nest, or Really, Nest's Data." Ars Technica. January 15, 2014. Accessed October 06, 2017. http://arstechnica.com/business/2014/01/what-google-can-really-do-with-nest-or-really-nests-data/.

Jouvenal, Justin. "Commit a Crime? Your Fitbit, Key Fob or Pacemaker Could Snitch on You." The Washington Post. October 09, 2017. Accessed October 14, 2017. https://www.washingtonpost.com/local/public-safety/commit-a-crime-your-fitbit-key-fob-or-pacemaker-could-snitch-on-you/2017/10/09/f35a4f30-8f50-11e7-8df5-c2e5cf46c1e2_story.html?utm_term=.e5d160467e23&wpisrc=nl_mustreads&wpmm=1.

Jouvenal, Justin. "Police Are Using Software to Predict Crime. Is It a 'holy Grail' Or Biased against Minorities?" The Washington Post. November 17, 2016. Accessed October 20, 2017. https://www.washingtonpost.com/local/public-safety/police-are-using-software-to-predict-crime-is-it-a-holy-grail-or-biased-against-minori-

ties/2016/11/17/525a6649-0472-440a-aae1-b283aa8e5de8_story.
html?utm_term=.749064b2033e.

Kenwright, Stephen. "The Antisocial Network: Path Texts
My Entire Phonebook at 6am." Branded3. October 09, 2013.
Accessed October 14, 2017. https://www.branded3.com/blog/
the-antisocial-network-path-texts-my-entire-phonebook-at-6am/.

Kharpal, Arjun. "Verizon Completes Its $4.48 Billion Acquisition
of Yahoo; Marissa Mayer Leaves with $23 Million." CNBC. June 13,
2017. Accessed October 22, 2017. https://www.cnbc.com/2017/06/13/
verizon-completes-yahoo-acquisition-marissa-mayer-resigns.html.

Kitchen, Martin. "The German Invasion of Canada in
the First World War." The International History Review
7, no. 2 (May 01, 1985): 245-60. http://www.jstor.org/
stable/40105462?seq=1#page_scan_tab_contents.

Kobie, Nicole. "Researchers Claim Facebook Tracks You Even
If You Opt Out." Motherboard. March 31, 2015. Accessed
October 12, 2017. http://motherboard.vice.com/read/
researchers-claim-facebook-tracks-you-even-if-you-opt-out.

Kohler, Carson. "We Heard Social Media Can Affect Your Credit
Score. Here." The Penny Hoarder. August 30, 2017. Accessed
October 06, 2017. https://www.thepennyhoarder.com/smart-money/
what-affects-your-credit-score/.

Kolbert, Elizabeth. "Why Facts Don't Change Our Minds."
The New Yorker. June 19, 2017. Accessed October 12,
2017. https://www.newyorker.com/magazine/2017/02/27/
why-facts-dont-change-our-minds.

Kollewe, Julia. "Google and Facebook Bring in One-fifth of Global
Ad Revenue." The Guardian. May 01, 2017. Accessed October
06, 2017. https://www.theguardian.com/media/2017/may/02/

google-and-facebook-bring-in-one-fifth-of-global-ad-revenue.

Kornblum, Anet. "AOL Dumps New Member Policy - CNET News." CNET. July 29, 1997. Accessed October 11, 2017. http://archive.is/GPPzv.

Kravets, David. "An Intentional Mistake: The Anatomy of Google's Wi-Fi Sniffing Debacle." Wired. June 03, 2017. Accessed October 11, 2017. http://www.wired.com/2012/05/google-wifi-fcc-investigation/.

Krebs, Brian. "Krebs on Security." Krebs on Security RSS. February 14, 2014. Accessed October 12, 2017. http://krebsonsecurity.com/2014/02/target-hackers-broke-in-via-hvac-company/.

Kushner, David. "The Darknet: The Battle for 'the Wild West of the Internet'." Rolling Stone. October 22, 2015. Accessed October 12, 2017. http://www.rollingstone.com/politics/news/the-battle-for-the-dark-net-20151022?page=2.

LaFrance, Adrienne. "How Self-Driving Cars Will Threaten Privacy." The Atlantic. March 21, 2016. Accessed October 06, 2017. https://www.theatlantic.com/technology/archive/2016/03/self-driving-cars-and-the-looming-privacy-apocalypse/474600/.

Lanier, Jaron. Who Owns the Future? London: Penguin Books, 2014.

Lapowsky, Issie. "The Real Trouble With Trump's 'Dark Post' Facebook Ads." Wired. September 20, 2017. Accessed October 09, 2017. https://www.wired.com/story/trump-dark-post-facebook-ads/.

Larson, Jeff, and Julia Angwin. "NSA Spying Relies on AT&T's 'Extreme Willingness to Help'." ProPublica. August 15, 2015. Accessed October 05, 2017. https://www.propublica.org/article/nsa-spying-relies-on-atts-extreme-willingness-to-help.

Larson, Selena. "Every Single Yahoo Account Was Hacked."
CNNMoney. October 4, 2017. Accessed October 10, 2017. http://
money.cnn.com/2017/10/03/technology/business/yahoo-breach-3-
billion-accounts/index.html.

Lobosco, Katie. "Facebook Friends Could Change Your Credit Score."
CNNMoney. August 27, 2013. Accessed October 06, 2017. http://
money.cnn.com/2013/08/26/technology/social/facebook-credit-score/.

Madden, Mary, and Lee Rainie. "Americans' Attitudes
About Privacy, Security and Surveillance." Pew Research
Center: Internet, Science & Tech. May 20, 2015. Accessed
October 05, 2017. http://www.pewinternet.org/2015/05/20/
americans-attitudes-about-privacy-security-and-surveillance/.

Matyszczyk, Chris. "Samsung Changes Smart TV Privacy
Policy in Wake of Spying Fears." CNET. February 10, 2015.
Accessed October 11, 2017. http://www.cnet.com/news/
samsung-changes-smarttv-privacy-policy-in-wake-of-spying-fears/.

Mayer-Schoǐ^nberger, Viktor, and Kenneth Cukier. Big Data a
Revolution That Will Transform How We Live, Work and Think.
Boston: Mariner Books, 2014.

Mearian, Lucas. "Insurance Company Now Offers Discounts -- If You
Let It Track Your Fitbit." Computerworld. April 17, 2015. Accessed
October 06, 2017. http://www.computerworld.com/article/2911594/
insurance-company-now-offers-discounts-if-you-let-it-track-your-
fitbit.html.

Michael, Paul. "Retail Tracking Technology Through Wifi, Loyalty
Programs | Money." Time. September 23, 2016. Accessed October 10,
2017. http://time.com/money/4506297/how-retailers-track-you/.

Mills, Chris. "Media Giant Viacom Dodges Bullet over
Massive Security Breach." BGR. September 19, 2017.

Accessed October 11, 2017. http://bgr.com/2017/09/19/
viacom-data-leak-security-firm-upguard/.

"Mobile Fact Sheet." Pew Research Center: Internet, Science & Tech.
January 12, 2017. Accessed October 10, 2017. http://www.pewinternet.
org/fact-sheet/mobile/.

Monroe, Randall. "Password Strength." Xkcd: Password Strength.
Accessed October 11, 2017. https://xkcd.com/936/.

Morran, Chris. "PayPal's New Terms Of Service Mean More
Robocalls, Spam Texts For Users." Consumerist. September 27, 2016.
Accessed October 11, 2017. http://consumerist.com/2015/06/02/
PayPals-new-terms-of-service-mean-more-robocalls-spam-texts-for-
users/.

Murphy, Margi. "Woman's Hacked Webcam Tells Her
to 'suck My D—'." New York Post. October 06, 2017.
Accessed October 08, 2017. http://nypost.com/2017/10/06/
womans-hacked-webcam-tells-her-to-suck-my-d/.

Newman, Lily Hay. "Equifax Officially Has No Excuse." Wired.
September 14, 2017. Accessed October 11, 2017. https://www.wired.
com/story/equifax-breach-no-excuse/.

Newman, Lily Hay. "Here's the Company That Caused the Target
Hack ." Slate Magazine. February 06, 2014. Accessed October
12, 2017. http://www.slate.com/blogs/future_tense/2014/02/06/
the_target_hackers_got_credentials_from_hvac_and_refrigera-
tion_company_fazio.html.

Nguyen, Peter. "8 Utterly Terrifying Things Hackers Can
Do With Your Personal Info." What Hackers Do with
Your Personal Information. March 07, 2014. Accessed
October 12, 2017. http://blog.hotspotshield.com/2014/03/07/
things-hackers-can-do-with-your-info/.

Nicks, Denver. "LinkedIn to Pay Out $13 M in Spam Settlement." Time. October 6, 2015. Accessed October 14, 2017. http://time.com/4062519/linkedn-spam-settlement/.

Nield, David. "How to Use Signal and Keep Your Chat Safe With Encryption." Popular Mechanics. March 28, 2017. Accessed October 12, 2017. http://www.popularmechanics.com/technology/apps/a25736/signal-app-guide-how-to-use/.

Perrin, Andrew. "Social Media Usage: 2005-2015." Pew Research Center: Internet, Science & Tech. October 08, 2015. Accessed October 22, 2017. http://www.pewinternet.org/2015/10/08/social-networking-usage-2005-2015/.

Peterson, Andrea. "Yes, Terrorists Could Have Hacked Dick Cheney's Heart." The Washington Post. October 21, 2013. Accessed October 06, 2017. https://www.washingtonpost.com/news/the-switch/wp/2013/10/21/yes-terrorists-could-have-hacked-dick-cheneys-heart/?utm_term=.8b6d4e86dc69.

Pham, Tam. "20 Ruthless Companies Who Lied, Spammed, and Deceived Us to Grow Their Business in the Early Days." The Hustle. February 24, 2016. Accessed October 14, 2017. https://thehustle.co/ruthless-companies-who-lied-spammed-and-deceived-users-to-grow-their-company-in-the-early-days.

Poulsen, Kevin. "Google Takes Wi-Fi Snooping Scandal to the Supreme Court." Wired. April 01, 2014. Accessed October 11, 2017. http://www.wired.com/2014/04/threatlevel_0401_streetview/.

Rawlinson, Kevin. "Tesco Accused of Using Electronic Armbands to Monitor Its Staff." The Independent. February 13, 2013. Accessed October 10, 2017. http://www.independent.co.uk/news/business/news/tesco-accused-of-using-electronic-armbands-to-monitor-its-staff-8493952.html.

Read, Max. "The Creepy Company Compiling a File on Your
Online Activity-Using Your Real Name." Gawker. October 25, 2010.
Accessed October 06, 2017. http://gawker.com/5672370/the-creepy-
company-compiling-a-file-on-your-online-activityusing-your-real-
name.

Richards, Katie. "Study: Ad Industry Accounted for 19 Percent of
US GDP in 2014." – Adweek. November 17, 2015. Accessed October
06, 2017. http://www.adweek.com/news/advertising-branding/
study-ad-industry-contributed-nearly-20-percent-toward-us-
gdp-2014-168164.

Robb, David. "Pennsylvania Man Pleads Guilty to Hacking
Celebrity Computers." Deadline. May 24, 2016. Accessed October
23, 2017. http://deadline.com/2016/05/celebrity-email-hack-
er-pleads-guilty-ryan-collins-jennifer-lawrence-1201762066/.

Roberts, Jeff. "Deloitte Gets Hacked: What We Know So Far."
Fortune. September 25, 2017. Accessed October 11, 2017. http://
fortune.com/2017/09/25/deloitte-hack/.

Rossignol, Joe. "IPhone Ownership Reaches All-Time High
in United States." Mac Rumors. April 20, 2017. Accessed
October 10, 2017. https://www.macrumors.com/2017/04/20/
iphone-ownership-all-time-high-us/.

Schaub, Florian. "Nobody Reads Privacy Policies – Here's
How to Fix That." The Conversation. October 11, 2017.
Accessed October 11, 2017. https://theconversation.com/
nobody-reads-privacy-policies-heres-how-to-fix-that-81932.

Schmidt, Michael S. "Racy Photos Were Often Shared at N.S.A.,
Snowden Says." The New York Times. July 20, 2014. Accessed
October 09, 2017. https://www.nytimes.com/2014/07/21/us/politics/
edward-snowden-at-nsa-sexually-explicit-photos-often-shared.
html?_r=0.

Selyukh, Alina. "The FBI Has Successfully Unlocked The IPhone Without Apple's Help." NPR. March 28, 2016. Accessed October 09, 2017. http://www.npr.org/sections/thetwo-way/2016/03/28/472192080/the-fbi-has-successfully-unlocked-the-iphone-without-apples-help.

Sengupta, Somini. "No US Action, So States Move on Privacy Law." The New York Times. October 30, 2013. Accessed October 14, 2017. http://www.nytimes.com/2013/10/31/technology/no-us-action-so-states-move-on-privacy-law.html.

Shields, Todd. "Mattel Gadget Listens to Babies, Setting Off Privacy Alarms." Bloomberg.com. September 29, 2017. Accessed October 06, 2017. https://www.bloomberg.com/news/articles/2017-09-29/mattel-nursery-gadget-listens-to-babies-sets-off-privacy-alarms.

Sisario, Ben. "Spotify Is Growing, but So Are Its Losses." The New York Times. June 15, 2017. Accessed October 11, 2017. https://www.nytimes.com/2017/06/15/business/media/streaming-radio-spotify-pandora.html.

Smith, Aaron, and Monica Anderson. "1. Online Shopping and Purchasing Preferences." Pew Research Center: Internet, Science & Tech. December 19, 2016. Accessed October 12, 2017. http://www.pewinternet.org/2016/12/19/online-shopping-and-purchasing-preferences/.

Smithers, Rebecca. "Terms and Conditions: Not Reading the Small Print Can Mean Big Problems." The Guardian. May 11, 2011. Accessed October 11, 2017. http://www.theguardian.com/money/2011/may/11/terms-conditions-small-print-big-problems.

Snyder, Chris, and Alex Heath. "A Security Expert Explains Why You Should Put Tape over Your Laptop Camera." Business Insider. December 07, 2016. Accessed October 04, 2017. http://www.businessinsider.com/why-you-should-put-tape-over-laptop-camera-2016-12.

Soergel, Andrew. "Morgan Stanley Says Ex-Employee Behind Data Breach." US News. January 6, 2015. Accessed October 12, 2017. http://www.usnews.com/news/newsgram/articles/2015/01/06/former-morgan-stanley-employee-accused-of-stealing-350-000-clients-account-information.

Somers, James. "Progress in AI Seems like It's Accelerating, but Here's Why It Could Be Plateauing." MIT Technology Review. October 04, 2017. Accessed October 06, 2017. https://www.technologyreview.com/s/608911/is-ai-riding-a-one-trick-pony/. "The State of Retail Report 2017." TimeTrade. Accessed October 11, 2017. http://www.timetrade.com/news/press-releases/study-85-consumers-prefer-shop-physical-stores-vs-online.

Sterling, Greg. "Echo and Home Will Probably Have to Tell You They're Always Listening -- in Europe." Search Engine Land. October 11, 2017. Accessed October 11, 2017. https://searchengineland.com/echo-home-will-probably-tell-theyre-always-listening-europe-284435.

Strauss, Valerie. "Report: Big Education Firms Spend Millions Lobbying for Pro-testing Policies." The Washington Post. March 30, 2015. Accessed October 04, 2017. https://www.washingtonpost.com/news/answer-sheet/wp/2015/03/30/report-big-education-firms-spend-millions-lobbying-for-pro-testing-policies/?utm_term=.405a67ad63b1.

Streitfeld, David. "Google Concedes That Drive-By Prying Violated Privacy." The New York Times. March 12, 2013. Accessed October 11, 2017. http://www.nytimes.com/2013/03/13/technology/google-pays-fine-over-street-view-privacy-breach.html?pagewanted=all.

Taylor, Adam. "Analysis | American Voter Turnout Is Still Lower than Most Other Wealthy Nations." The Washington Post. November 10, 2016. Accessed October 10, 2017. https://www.washingtonpost.com/news/worldviews/wp/2016/11/10/

even-in-a-historic-election-americans-dont-vote-as-much-as-those-from-other-nations/?utm_term=.e86e6b0d3d8f.

TowerData. "TowerData News." News. Accessed October 06, 2017. http://www.towerdata.com/company/news/towerdata-acquires-rapleaf-press-release.

Tran, Kevin. "YouTube Touts Effectiveness of Six-second Ads." Business Insider. September 18, 2017. Accessed October 14, 2017. http://www.businessinsider.com/youtube-touts-effectiveness-of-six-second-ads-2017-9.

Tsukayama, Hayley. "Mattel Has Canceled Plans for a Kid-focused AI Device That Drew Privacy Concerns." The Washington Post. October 04, 2017. Accessed October 06, 2017. https://www.washingtonpost.com/news/the-switch/wp/2017/10/04/mattel-has-an-ai-device-to-soothe-babies-experts-are-begging-them-not-to-sell-it/?utm_term=.b2f3e39fa1df.

UC Santa Barbara. "Woodrow Wilson: Third Annual Message - December 7, 1915." The American Presidency Project. Accessed October 04, 2017. http://www.presidency.ucsb.edu/ws/index.php?pid=29556.

Volz, Dustin. "Uber to End Post-trip Tracking of Riders as Part of Privacy Push." Reuters. August 29, 2017. Accessed October 11, 2017. https://www.reuters.com/article/us-uber-privacy/uber-to-end-post-trip-tracking-of-riders-as-part-of-privacy-push-idUSKCN1B90EN.

Ward, Mark. "It Is Easy to Expose Users' Secret Web Habits, Say Researchers." BBC News. July 31, 2017. Accessed October 06, 2017. http://www.bbc.com/news/technology-40770393.
Weigend, Andreas S. Data for the People: How to Make Our Post-privacy Economy Work for You. New York: Basic Books, 2017.

White, Christopher. "Dropbox Can Legally Sell All of Your Files

[Update]." Neowin. July 02, 2011. Accessed October 14, 2017. https://www.neowin.net/news/dropbox-legally-owns-all-of-your-files.

"Why Do We Blindly Sign Terms Of Service Agreements?" NPR. September 01, 2014. Accessed October 11, 2017. http://www.npr.org/2014/09/01/345044359/why-do-we-blindly-sign-terms-of-service-agreements.

"Why It's Time to Say Goodbye to IKTHTMISOAIW." WPP Annual Report and Accounts 2013 - Why It's Time to Say Goodbye to IKTHTMISOAIW. Accessed October 06, 2017. http://www.wpp.com/annualreports/2013/what-we-think/why-its-time-to-say-goodbye-to-ikthtmisoaiw/.

"WikiLeaks Publishes Second Batch of Docs from CIA Chief's Personal Email." RT International. October 22, 15. Accessed October 12, 2017. https://www.rt.com/usa/319424-wikileaks-publishes-brennan-email/.

Wong, Raymond. "Apple Commercial Reminds Us Why Siri Needs The Rock More than The Rock Needs Siri." Mashable. July 24, 2017. Accessed October 14, 2017. http://mashable.com/2017/07/24/the-rock-apple-siri-movie-why-digital-assistants-suck/#gSsiZpLs-BPqj.

Writer, Ken Sweet Ap Business. "Equifax: 2.5 Million More Americans May Be Affected by Hack." ABC News. October 2, 2017. Accessed October 10, 2017. http://abcnews.go.com/Technology/wireStory/equifax-25-million-americans-affected-hack-50240314.

"Yellow Journalism." PBS. Accessed October 14, 2017. https://www.pbs.org/crucible/frames/_journalism.html.

Yuhas, Alan. "Snapchat Accused of Lying about User Numbers to Inflate Value of IPO." The Guardian. January 05, 2017. Accessed October 22, 2017. https://www.theguardian.com/technology/2017/

jan/05/snapchat-accused-lying-user-numbers-ipo-investors.

Zetter, Kim. "Is Anonymous Dead, or Just Preparing to Rise Again?" Wired. June 03, 2017. Accessed October 12, 2017. http://www.wired.com/2014/06/anonymous-sabu/.

Zipkin, Nina. "Get This: Sony Hack Reveals Company Stored Passwords in Folder Labeled 'Password'." Entrepreneur. December 05, 2014. Accessed October 12, 2017. http://www.entrepreneur.com/article/240517.

PRIVACY

AND HOW TO GET
IT BACK BY B. J.
MENDELSON WAS ED
ITED IN LONDON IN
OCTOBER 2017. TYPE
SET IN MINION PRO

CURIOUS READS …are short books that connect the dots on topics that matter; topics everyone reads about, hears about, and talks about. Written by subject-matter experts for nonspecialist readers, they are accessible, concise, and beautifully produced.

ALSO OUT IN FALL 2017

Spies: Treachery, Secrecy, Paranoia
Paula Schmitt

Vampires: Lovesick & Bloodthirsty
Justin E. H. Smith

Water Wars: Fight to the Last Drop
Frederika Whitehead

Immortality: Live Forever or Die Trying
Guy Weress

www.curiousreads.net

Prospect Heights Public Library
12 N. Elm Street
Prospect Heights, IL 60070
www.phpl.info